T0210610

Vision-Based Interaction

Synthesis Lectures on Computer Vision

Editor
Gérard Medioni, *University of Southern California*
Sven Dicksinson, *University of Toronto*

Synthesis Lectures on Computer Vision is edited by Gérard Medioni of the University of Southern California and Sven Dickinson of the University of Toronto. The series will publish 50- to 150 page publications on topics pertaining to computer vision and pattern recognition. The scope will largely follow the purview of premier computer science conferences, such as ICCV, CVPR, and ECCV. Potential topics include, but not are limited to:

- Applications and Case Studies for Computer Vision

- Color, Illumination, and Texture

- Computational Photography and Video

- Early and Biologically-inspired Vision

- Face and Gesture Analysis

- Illumination and Reflectance Modeling

- Image-Based Modeling

- Image and Video Retrieval

- Medical Image Analysis

- Motion and Tracking

- Object Detection, Recognition, and Categorization

- Segmentation and Grouping

- Sensors

- Shape-from-X

- Stereo and Structure from Motion

- Shape Representation and Matching

- Statistical Methods and Learning

- Performance Evaluation

- Video Analysis and Event Recognition

Vision-Based Interaction
Matthew Turk and Gang Hua
2013

Camera Networks: The Acquisition and Analysis of Videos over Wide Areas
Amit K. Roy-Chowdhury and Bi Song
2012

Deformable Surface 3D Reconstruction from Monocular Images
Mathieu Salzmann and Pascal Fua
2010

Boosting-Based Face Detection and Adaptation
Cha Zhang and Zhengyou Zhang
2010

Image-Based Modeling of Plants and Trees
Sing Bing Kang and Long Quan
2009

Vision-Based Interaction
Matthew Turk and Gang Hua

ISBN: 978-3-031-00684-5 paperback
ISBN: 978-3-031-01812-1 ebook

DOI: 10.1007/978-3-031-01812-1

A Publication in the Springer series
SYNTHESIS LECTURES ON COMPUTER VISION

Lecture #5
Series Editors: Gérard Medioni, *University of Southern California*
              Sven Dickinson, *University of Toronto*
Series ISSN
Synthesis Lectures on Computer Vision
Print 2153-1056   Electronic 2153-1064

Vision–Based Interaction

Matthew Turk
University of California, Santa Barbara

Gang Hua
Stevens Institute of Technology

SYNTHESIS LECTURES ON COMPUTER VISION #5

ABSTRACT

In its early years, the field of computer vision was largely motivated by researchers seeking computational models of biological vision and solutions to practical problems in manufacturing, defense, and medicine. For the past two decades or so, there has been an increasing interest in computer vision as an input modality in the context of human-computer interaction. Such *vision-based interaction* can endow interactive systems with visual capabilities similar to those important to human-human interaction, in order to perceive non-verbal cues and incorporate this information in applications such as interactive gaming, visualization, art installations, intelligent agent interaction, and various kinds of command and control tasks. Enabling this kind of rich, visual and multimodal interaction requires interactive-time solutions to problems such as detecting and recognizing faces and facial expressions, determining a person's direction of gaze and focus of attention, tracking movement of the body, and recognizing various kinds of gestures.

In building technologies for vision-based interaction, there are choices to be made as to the range of possible sensors employed (e.g., single camera, stereo rig, depth camera), the precision and granularity of the desired outputs, the mobility of the solution, usability issues, etc. Practical considerations dictate that there is not a one-size-fits-all solution to the variety of interaction scenarios; however, there are principles and methodological approaches common to a wide range of problems in the domain. While new sensors such as the Microsoft Kinect are having a major influence on the research and practice of vision-based interaction in various settings, they are just a starting point for continued progress in the area.

In this book, we discuss the landscape of history, opportunities, and challenges in this area of vision-based interaction; we review the state-of-the-art and seminal works in detecting and recognizing the human body and its components; we explore both static and dynamic approaches to "looking at people" vision problems; and we place the computer vision work in the context of other modalities and multimodal applications. Readers should gain a thorough understanding of current and future possibilities of computer vision technologies in the context of human-computer interaction.

KEYWORDS

computer vision, vision-based interaction, perceptual interface, face and gesture recognition, movement analysis

MT: To K, H, M, and L

GH: To Yan and Kayla, and my family

Contents

Preface xi

Acknowledgments xiii

Figure Credits xv

1   Introduction **1**
   1.1   Problem definition and terminology 1
   1.2   VBI motivation 4
   1.3   A brief history of VBI 4
   1.4   Opportunities and challenges for VBI 9
   1.5   Organization 9

2   Awareness: Detection and Recognition **11**
   2.1   What to detect and recognize? 12
   2.2   Review of state-of-the-art and seminal works 14
        2.2.1   Face 15
        2.2.2   Eyes 35
        2.2.3   Hands 39
        2.2.4   Full body 42
   2.3   Contextual human sensing 45

3   Control: Visual Lexicon Design for Interaction **47**
   3.1   Static visual information 48
        3.1.1   Lexicon design from body/hand posture 48
        3.1.2   Lexicon design from face/head/facial expression 52
        3.1.3   Lexicon design from eye gaze 54
   3.2   Dynamic visual information 55
        3.2.1   Model-based approaches 56
        3.2.2   Exemplar-based approaches 60
   3.3   Combining static and dynamic visual information 62
        3.3.1   The SWP systems 63

      3.3.2 The VM system 64

  3.4   Discussions and remarks 65

4   **Multimodal Integration** **67**

  4.1   Joint audio-visual analysis 69

  4.2   Vision and touch/haptics 70

  4.3   Multi-sensor fusion 71

5   **Applications of Vision-Based Interaction** **73**

  5.1   Application scenarios for VBI 73

  5.2   Commercial systems 76

6   **Summary and Future Directions** **81**

  Bibliography **85**

  Authors' Biographies **115**

Preface

Like many areas of computing, vision-based interaction has found motivation and inspiration from authors and filmmakers who have painted compelling pictures of future technology. From *2001: A Space Odyssey* to *The Terminator* to *Minority Report* to *Iron Man*, audiences have seen computers interacting with people visually in natural, human-like ways: recognizing people, understanding their facial expressions, appreciating their artwork, measuring their body size and shape, and responding to gestures. While this often works out badly for the humans in these stories, presumably this is not the fault of the interface, and in many cases these futuristic visions suggest useful and desirable technologies to pursue.

Perusing the proceedings of the top computer vision conferences over the years shows just how much the idea of computers looking at people has influenced the field. In the early 1990s, a relatively small number of papers had images of people in them, while the vast majority had images of generic objects, automobiles, aerial views, buildings, hallways, and laboratories. (Notably, there were many papers back then with no images at all!) In addition, computer vision work was typically only seen in computer vision conferences. Nowadays, conference papers are full of images of people—not all in the context of interaction, but for a wide range of scenarios where people are the main focus of the problems being addressed—and computer vision methods and technologies appear in a variety of other research venues, especially including CHI (human-computer interaction), SIGGRAPH (computer graphics and interactive techniques) and multimedia conferences, as well as conferences devoted exclusively to these and related topics, such as FG (face and gesture recognition) and ICMI (multimodal interaction). It seems reasonable to say that people have become a main focus (if not *the* main focus) of computer vision research and applications.

Part of the reason for this is the significant growth in consumer-oriented computer vision—solutions that provide tools to improve picture taking, organizing personal media, gaming, exercise, etc. Cameras now find faces, wait for the subjects to smile, and do automatic color balancing to make sure the skin looks about right. Services allow users to upload huge amounts of image and video data and then automatically identify friends and family members and link to related stored images and video. Video games now track multiple players and provide live feedback on performance, calorie burn, and such. These consumer-oriented applications of computer vision are just getting started; the field is poised to contribute in many diverse and significant ways in the years to come. An additional benefit for those of us who have been in the field for a while is that we can finally explain to our relatives what we do, without the associated blank stares.

The primary goals of this book are to present a bird's eye view of vision-based interaction, to provide insight into the core problems, opportunities, and challenges, and to supply a snapshot of key methods and references at this particular point in time.

While the machines are still on our side.

Matthew Turk and Gang Hua
September 2013

Acknowledgments

We would firstly like to thank Gerard Medioni and Sven Dickinson, the editors of this Synthesis Lectures on Computer Vision series, for inviting us to contribute to the series. We are grateful to the reviewers, who provided us with constructive feedback that made the book better. We would also like to thank all the people who granted us permission to use their figures in this book. Without their contribution, it would have been much more difficult for us to complete the manuscript. We greatly appreciate the support, patience, and help of our editor, Diane Cerra, at every phase of writing this book. Last but not least, we would like to thank our families for their love and support.

We would like to acknowledge partial support from the National Science Foundation.

Matthew Turk and Gang Hua
September 2013

Figure Credits

Figures 1.2 a, b	from *2001: A Space Odyssey*, 1968. Metro-Goldwyn-Mayer Inc., 3 April 1968; LP36136 (in copyright registry) Copyright © Renewed 1996 by Turner Entertainment Company.
Figure 1.2 c	from *The Terminator*, 1984. Copyright © 2011 by Annapurna Pictures.
Figure 1.2 d	from *Minority Report*, 2002. Copyright © 2002 BY Dreamworks LLC and Twentieth Century Fox Film Corporation.
Figures 1.2 e, f	from *Iron Man*, 2008. Copyright © 2008 by Marvel.
Figures 1.3 a, b	from Myron Krueger, *Videoplace*, 1970. Used with permission.
Figures 1.4 a, b	courtesy of Irfan Essa.
Figures 1.4 c, d	courtesy of Jim Davis
Figures 1.4 e, f	courtesy of Christopher Wren
Figures 2.2 a, b and 2.3	based on Viola, et al: Rapid object detection using a boosted cascade of simple features. *Proceedings of the IEEE Conference on Computer Vision and Pattern Recognition 2001*, volume 1, pages 511-518. Copyright © 2001 IEEE. Adapted courtesy of Viola, P. A. and Jones, M. J.
Figures 2.4 a, b, c, d, e, f, g and 2.5	from Hua, et al: A robust elastic and partial matching metric for face recognition. *Proceedings of the IEEE International Conference on Computer Vision, 2009*. Copyright © 2009 IEEE. Used with permission.
Figure 2.12	based on Song, et al: Learning universal multi-view age estimator by video contexts. *Proceedings of the IEEE International Conference on Computer Vision, 2011*. Copyright © 2011 IEEE. Adapted courtesy of Song, Z., Ni, B., Guo, D., Sim, T., and Yan, S.
Figure 2.13	from Jesorsky, et al: Robust face detection using the hausdorff distance. *Audio- and Video-Based Biometric Person Authentication: Proceedings of the Third International Conference, AVBPA 2001 Halmstad, Sweden, June 6–8, 2001*, pages 90-95. Copyright © 2001, Springer-Verlag Berlin Heidelberg. Used with permission. DOI: 10.1007/3-540-45344-X_14

Figure 2.14   based on Chen, J. and Ji, Q. Probabilistic gaze estimation without active personal calibration. *Proceedings of the IEEE Conference on Computer Vision and Pattern Recognition, 2011.* Copyright © 2011 IEEE. Adapted courtesy of Chen, J. and Ji, Q.

Figures 2.15 **a, b, c, d, e**   from Mittal, et al: Hand detection using multiple proposals. *British Machine Vision Conference, 2011.* Copyright and all rights therein are retained by authors. Used courtesy of Mittal, A., Zisserman, A., and Torr, P. H. S. http://www.robots.ox.ac.uk/~vgg/publications/2011/Mittal11/

Figure 2.16   Wachs, et al: Vision-based hand-gesture applications. *Communications of the ACM*, 54(2), 60-72. Copyright © 2011, Association for Computing Machinery, Inc. Reprinted by permission. DOI: 10.1145/1897816.1897838

Figure 2.17   from Felzenszwalb, et al: Object detection with discriminatively trained part-based models. *IEEE Transactions on Pattern Analysis and Machine Intelligence*, 32(9), 1627-1645. Copyright © 2010 IEEE. Used with permission. DOI: 10.1109/TPAMI.2009.167

Figure 2.18   from Codasign. *Skeleton tracking with the kinect.* Used with permission. URL: http://learning.codasign.com/index.php?title=Skeleton_Tracking_with_the_Kinect

Figure 3.1   from *Kinect Rush: A Disney Pixar Adventure.* Copyright © 2012 Microsoft Studio.

Figure 3.2   from Freeman, et al: Television control by hand gestures. *IEEE International Workshop on Automatic Face and Gesture Recognition, Zurich.* Copyright © 1995 IEEE. Used with permission.

Figures 3.3 **a, b**   from Iannizzotto, et al: A vision-based user interface for real-time controlling toy cars. *10th IEEE Conference on Emerging Technologies and Factory Automation, 2005 (ETFA 2005)*, volume 1. Copyright © 2005 IEEE. Used with permission.

Figure 3.4   from Stenger, et al: A vision-based remote control. In R. Cipolla, S. Battiato, and G. Farinella (Eds.), *Computer Vision: Detection, Recognition and Reconstruction*, pages 233-262. Springer Berlin / Heidelberg. Copyright © 2010, Springer-Verlag Berlin Heidelberg. Used with permission. DOI: 10.1007/978-3-642-12848-69

Figures 3.5 a, b   from Tu, et al: Face as mouse through visual face tracking. *Computer Vision and Image Understanding*, 108(1-2), 35-40. Copyright © 2007 Elsevier Inc. Reprinted with permission. DOI: 10.1016/j.cviu.2006.11.007

Figure 3.6 a   from Marcel, et al: Hand gesture recognition using input-output hidden markov models. *Proceedings of the Fourth IEEE International Conference on Automatic Face and Gesture Recognition, 2000*. Copyright © 2000 IEEE. Used with permission. DOI: 10.1109/AFGR.2000.840674

Figure 3.6 b   based on Marcel, et al: Hand gesture recognition using input-output hidden markov models. *Proceedings of the Fourth IEEE International Conference on Automatic Face and Gesture Recognition, 2000*. Copyright © 2000 IEEE. Adapted courtesy of Marcel, S., Bernier, O., and Collobert, D. DOI: 10.1109/AFGR.2000.840674

Figure 3.7   based on Rajko, et al: Real-time gesture recognition with minimal training requirements and on-line learning. *IEEE Conference on Computer Vision and Pattern Recognition, 2007*. Copyright © 2007 IEEE. Adapted courtesy of Rajko, S., Gang Qian, Ingalls, T., and James, J.

Figure 3.8 a   based on Elgammal, et al: Learning dynamics for exemplar-based gesture recognition. *Proceedings of the 2003 IEEE Computer Society Conference on Computer Vision and Pattern Recognition*. Copyright © 2003 IEEE. Adapted courtesy of Elgammal, A., Shet, V., Yacoob, Y., and Davis, L. S. DOI: 10.1109/CVPR.2003.1211405

Figure 3.8 b   from Elgammal, et al: Learning dynamics for exemplar-based gesture recognition. *Proceedings of the 2003 IEEE Computer Society Conference on Computer Vision and Pattern Recognition*. Copyright © 2003 IEEE. Used with permission. DOI: 10.1109/CVPR.2003.1211405

Figure 3.9   from Wang, et al: Hidden conditional random fields for gesture recognition. *2006 IEEE Computer Society Conference on Computer Vision and Pattern Recognition*. Copyright © 2006 IEEE. Used with permission. DOI: 10.1109/CVPR.2006.132

Figures 3.10 and 3.11 b   based on Shen, et al: (2012). Dynamic hand gesture recognition: An exemplar based approach from motion divergence fields. *Image and Vision Computing: Best of Automatic Face and Gesture Recognition 2011*, 30(3), 227-235. Copyright © 2011 Elsevier B.V. Adapted courtesy of Shen, X., Hua, G., Williams, L., and Wu, Y.

Figures 3.11 a, c   from Shen, et al: (2012). Dynamic hand gesture recognition: An exemplar based approach from motion divergence fields. *Image and Vision Computing: Best of Automatic Face and Gesture Recognition 2011*, 30(3), 227-235. Copyright © 2011 Elsevier B.V. Used courtesy of Shen, X., Hua, G., Williams, L., and Wu, Y.

Figure 3.12   based on Hua, et al: Peye: Toward a visual motion based perceptual interface for mobile devices. *Proceedings of the IEEE International Workshop on Human Computer Interaction 2007*, pages 39-48. Copyright © 2007 IEEE. Adapted courtesy of Hua, G., Yang, T.-Y., and Vasireddy, S.

Figures 3.13 a, b   from Starner, et al: Real-time American sign language recognition using desk and wearable computer based video. *IEEE Transactions on Pattern Analysis and Machine Intelligence*, 20(12), 1371-1375. Copyright © 1998 IEEE. Used with permission. DOI: 10.1109/34.735811

Figure 3.14   from Vogler et al: A framework for recognizing the simultaneous aspects of American sign language. *Computer Vision and Image Understanding*, 81(3), 358-384. Copyright © 2001 Academic Press. Used with permission.

Figure 3.15   based on Vogler et al: A framework for recognizing the simultaneous aspects of American sign language. *Computer Vision and Image Understanding*, 81(3), 358-384. Copyright © 2001 Academic Press. Adapted courtesy of Vogler, C. and Metaxas, D.

Figure 4.1   from Bolt, R. A. (1980). "Put-that-there": Voice and gesture at the graphics interface. *Proceeding SIGGRAPH '80 Proceedings of the 7th Annual Conference on Computer Graphics and Interactive Techniques*, pages 262-270. Copyright © 1980, Association for Computing Machinery, Inc. Reprinted by permission. DOI: 10.1145/800250.807503

Figure 4.2   from Sodhi, et al: Aireal: Interactive tactile experiences in free air. *ACM Transactions on Graphics (TOG) - SIGGRAPH 2013 Conference Proceedings*, 32(4), July 2013, Article No. 134. Copyright © 2013, Association for Computing Machinery, Inc. Reprinted by permission. DOI: 10.1145/2461912.2462007

Figure 5.1 a   Copyright © 2010 Microsoft Corporation. Used with permission.

Figure 5.1 b   courtesy Cynthia Breazeal.

Figure 5.2 d   Copyright ©2013 Microsoft Corporation. Used with permission.

CHAPTER 1

Introduction

Computer vision has come a long way since the 1963 dissertation by Larry Roberts at MIT [Roberts, 1963] that is often considered a seminal point in the birth of the field. Over the decades, research in computer vision has been motivated by a range of problems, including understanding the processes of biological vision, interpreting aerial and medical imagery, robot navigation, multimedia database indexing and retrieval, and 3D model construction. For the past two decades or so, there has been an increasing interest in applications of computer vision in human-computer interaction, particularly in systems that process images of people in order to determine identity, expression, body pose, gesture, and activity. In some of these cases, visual information is an input modality in a multimodal system, providing non-verbal cues to accompany speech input and perhaps touch-based interaction. In addition to the security and surveillance applications that drove some of the initial work in the area, these *vision-based interaction (VBI)* technologies are of interest in gaming, conversational interfaces, ubiquitous and wearable computing, interactive visualization, accessibility, and several other consumer-oriented application areas.

At a high level, the goal of vision-based interaction is to perceive visual cues about people that may be useful to human-human interaction, in order to support more natural human-computer interaction. When interacting with another person, we may attend to several kinds of nonverbal visual cues, such as presence, location, identity, age, gender, race, body language, focus of attention, lip movements, gestures, and overall activity. The VBI challenge is to use sensor-based computer vision techniques to robustly and accurately detect, model, and recognize such visual cues, possibly integrating with additional sensing modalities, and to interact effectively with the semantics of the variety of applications that wish to leverage these capabilities.

In this book, we aim to describe some of the key methods and approaches in vision-based interaction and to discuss the state of the art in the field, providing both a historical perspective and a look toward the future in this area.

1.1 PROBLEM DEFINITION AND TERMINOLOGY

We define vision-based interaction (VBI) (also referred to as *looking at people*; see Pentland [2000]) as the use of real-time computer vision to support interactivity by detecting and recognizing people and their movements or activities. The sensor input to a VBI system may be one or more video cameras or depth sensors (using stereo or other 3D sensing technology). The environment may be tightly structured (e.g., controlled lighting and body positions, markers placed on the participant(s)), completely unstructured (e.g., no markers, no constraints on lighting, background objects, or movement), or something in between. Different scenarios may limit the input to particular body parts (e.g., the face, hands, upper body) or movements (e.g., subtle facial expressions, two-handed gestures, full-body motion).

Vision-based interaction may be used in the context of gaming, PC-based user interaction, mobile devices, virtual and mixed reality scenarios, and public installations, and in other settings, allowing for a wide range of target devices, problem constraints, and specific applications. In each of these contexts, key components of vision-based interaction include:

- Sensing – The capture of visual information from one or more sensors (and sensor types), and the initial steps toward detection, recognition, and tracking required to eventually create models of people and their actions.

- Awareness – Facilitating awareness of the user and key characteristics of the user (such as identity, location, and focus of attention) to help determine the context and the readiness of the user to interact with the system.

- Control – Estimating parameters (of expression, pose, gesture, and/or activity) intended for control or communication.

- Feedback – Presenting feedback (typically visual, audio, or haptic) that is useful and appropriate for the application context. This is not a VBI task per se, but an important component in any VBI system.

- Application interface – A mechanism for providing application-specific context to the system in order to guide the high-level goals and thus the processing requirements.

Figure 1.1 shows a generic view of these components and their relationships.

When sensing and perceiving people and their actions, it is helpful to be consistent with terminology to avoid confusion. The *pose* or *posture* of a person or a body component is the static configuration—i.e., the parameters (joint angles, facial action encoding, etc.) that define the relevant positions and orientations at a point in time. A *gesture* is a short duration, dynamic sequence of poses or postures that can be interpreted as a meaningful unit of communication. Thus making the peace (or victory) sign creates a posture, while waving goodbye makes a gesture. *Activity* typically refers to human movement over a longer period of time that may not have communicative intent or that may incorporate multiple movements and/or gestures.

In gesture recognition, unless the gestures are fixed to a particular point or duration in time (e.g., using a "push to gesture" functionality), it is necessary to determine when a dynamic gesture begins and ends. This temporal segmentation of gesture is a challenging problem, particularly in less constrained environments where several kinds of spontaneous gestures are possible amidst other movement not intended to communicate gestural information.

In the analysis and interpretation of facial expressions, the concepts of *expression* and *emotion* should be clearly distinguished. Facial expression (and also body pose) is an external visible

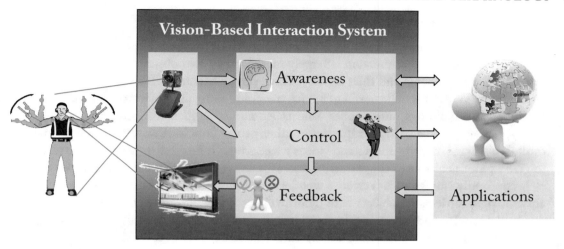

Figure 1.1: The three functional components of a system for vision-based interaction. The awareness and control components require vision processing, given application-specific constraints and goals. The feedback component is intended to communicate appropriate system information to the user.

signal that provides evidence for a person's emotional state, which is an internal, hidden variable. Expression and emotion do not have a one-to-one relationship—for example, someone may be smiling when angry or show a neutral expression when happy. In addition, facial gestures comprise expressions that may be completely unrelated to affect. So, despite a common trend in the literature, it is inaccurate to present facial expression recognition as classifying emotion—rather, it is classifying expression, which may provide some evidence (preferably along with other contextual information) for a subsequent classification of emotion (or other) states.

There is no clear agreement on the best nomenclature for describing human motion and its perception and modeling. Bobick [1997] provided a useful set of definitions several years ago. He defined *movement* as the most atomic primitive in motion perception, characterized by a space-time trajectory in a body kinematics-based configuration space. Recognition of movements is direct and requires no contextual information. Moving up the hierarchy, an *activity* refers to sequences of movements; in general, recognizing an activity requires knowledge about the constituent movements and the statistical properties of the temporal sequence of movements. Finally, an *action* is a larger-scale event that may include interactions with the environment and has a clear semantic interpretation in the particular context. Actions are thus at the boundary of perception and cognition. Perhaps unfortunately, this taxonomy of movement, activity, and action has not seen widespread adoption, and the terms (along with *motion*) tend to be used interchangeably and without clear distinction.

1.2   VBI MOTIVATION

In addition to general inspiration from literature and film (e.g., see Figure 1.2), the widespread interest in vision-based interaction is largely motivated by two observations. First, the focus is on understanding people and their activity, which can be beneficial in a wide variety of practical applications. While it is quite useful to model, track, and recognize objects such as airplanes, trees, machine parts, buildings, automobiles, landscapes, and other man-made and natural objects and scenes, humans have a particular interest in other people (and in themselves), and people play a central role in most of the images and videos we generate. It is not surprising that we would want to give a prominent role to the extracting and estimating visual information about people.

Secondly, human bodies create a wonderful challenge for computer vision methods. People are non-rigid, articulated objects with deformable components and widely varying appearances due to changes in clothing, hairstyle, facial hair, makeup, age, etc. In most recognition problems involving people, measures of the within-class differences (changes in visual appearance for a single person) can overwhelm the between-class differences (changes across different people), making simple classification schemes ineffective. Human movement is difficult to model precisely, due to the many kinematic degrees of freedom and the complex interaction among bones, muscles, skin, and clothing. At a higher level, human behavior relates the lower-level estimates of shape, size, and motion parameters to the semantics of communication and intent, creating a natural connect to the understanding of cognition and embodiment.

Vision-based interaction thus brings together opportunities both to solve deep problems in computer vision and artificial intelligence and to create practical systems that provide useful and desirable capabilities. By providing systems to detect people, recognize them, track their hands, arms, heads, and bodies, recognize their gestures, estimate their direction of gaze, recognize their facial expressions, or classify their activities, computer vision practitioners are creating solutions that have immediate applications in accessibility (making interaction feasible for people in a wide range of environments, including those with disabilities), entertainment, social interfaces, video-conferencing, speech recognition, biometrics, movement analysis, intelligent environments, and other areas. Along the way, research in the area pushes general-purpose computer vision and provides greater opportunities for integration with higher-level reasoning and artificial intelligence systems.

1.3   A BRIEF HISTORY OF VBI

Computer vision focusing on people seems to have begun with interest in automatic face recognition systems in the early days of the field. In 1966, Bledsoe [1966] wrote about man-machine facial recognition, and this was followed up with influential work by Kelly [1970], Kanade [1973], and Harmon et al. [1981]. In the late 1980s to early 1990s, work in face recognition began to blossom with a range of approaches introduced, including multiscale correlation [Burt, 1988], neural networks [Fleming and Cottrell, 1990], deformable feature models [Yuille et al., 1992],

Figure 1.2: Science fiction portrayals of vision-based interaction: (a) HAL's "eye" from *2001: A Space Odyssey*. (b) HAL appreciating the astronaut's sketch. (c) The cyborg's augmented reality view from *The Terminator*. (d) The gestural interface from *Minority Report*. (e) Gestural interaction and (f) facial analysis from *Iron Man*.

and subspace analysis approaches [Turk and Pentland, 1991a]. Although primarily motivated by (static) biometric considerations, face recognition technologies are important in interaction for establishing identity, which can introduce considerable contextual information to the interaction scenario.

In parallel to developments in face recognition, work in multimodal interfaces began to receive attention with the 1980 Put-That-There demonstration by Bolt [1980]. The system integrated voice and gesture inputs to enable a natural and efficient interaction with a wall display, part of a spatial data management system. The user could issue commands such as "create a blue square there," "make that smaller," "move that to the right of the yellow rectangle," and the canonical "put that there." None of these commands can be properly interpreted from either the audio or the gesture alone, but integrating the two cues eliminates the ambiguities of pronouns and spatial references and enables simple and natural communication. Since this seminal work, research in multimodal interaction has included several modalities (especially speech, vision, and haptics) and focused largely on "post-WIMP" [Van Dam, 1997] and perceptual interfaces [Oviatt and Cohen, 2000; Turk, 1998; Turk and Kölsch, 2004], of which computer vision detection, tracking, and recognition of people and their behavior is an integral part. The International Conference on Multimodal Interaction (ICMI), which began in 1996, highlights interdisciplinary research in this area.

Systems that used video-based interactivity for artistic exploration were pioneered by Myron Kreuger beginning in 1969, leading to the development of Videoplace in the mid-1970s through the 1980s. Videoplace (see Figure 1.3) was conceived as an artificial reality laboratory that surrounds the user and responds to movement in creative ways while projecting a live synthesized view in front of the user, like a virtual mirror. The user would see a silhouette of himself or herself along with artificial creatures, miniature views of the user, and other computer-generated elements in the scene, all interacting in meaningful ways. Although the computer vision aspects of the system were not very sophisticated, the use of vision and real-time image processing techniques in an interactive system was quite compelling and novel at the time. Over the years, the ACM SIGGRAPH conference has included a number of VBI-based systems of increasing capability for artistic exploration.

In the 1990s, the MIT Media Lab was a hotbed of activity for research in vision-based interaction, with continued work on face recognition [Pentland et al., 1994], facial expression analysis [Essa and Pentland, 1997], body modeling [Wren et al., 1997], gesture recognition [Darrell and Pentland, 1993; Starner and Pentland, 1997], human motion analysis [Davis and Bobick, 1997], and activity recognition [Bobick et al., 1997]. In 1994, the first Automatic Face and Gesture Recognition conference was held, which has been a primary destination for much of the work in this area since then.

The growth of commercial applications of vision-based interaction technologies in the past 10–15 years has been significant, starting with face recognition systems for biometric authentication and including face tracking for real-time character animation, marker- and LED-based body

(a)   (b)

Figure 1.3: Myron Kreuger's interactive Videoplace system, 1970. (a) Side view. (b) User views of the display.

tracking systems, head and face tracking for videoconferencing systems, body interaction systems for public installation, and camera-based sensing for gaming. The Sony EyeToy,[1] released in 2003 for the PlayStation 2, was the first successful consumer gaming camera to support user interaction through tracking and gesture recognition, selling over 10 million units. Its successor, the PlayStation Eye (for the Sony PS3), improved both camera quality and capabilities.

Another gaming device, the Microsoft Kinect,[2] which debuted in 2010 for the Xbox 360, has been a major milestone in commercial computer vision—and vision-based interaction in particular—selling approximately 25 million units in less than two and a half years. The Kinect is an RGBD (color video plus depth) camera, providing both video and depth information in real-time, including full-body motion capture, gesture recognition, and face recognition. Although limited to indoor use due to its use of near-infrared illumination and to a range of approximately 5–6 meters, people have found creative uses for the Kinect in a wide range of applications, well beyond its intent as a gaming device, including many applications of vision-based interaction.

A small device for sensing and tracking a user's fingers (all ten) for real-time gestural interaction, the Leap Motion Controller[3] was announced in 2012 and arrived on the commercial market in mid-2013. It supports hand-based gestures such as pointing, waving, reaching, and grabbing in an area directly above the sensor. The device has been highly anticipated and promises to enable a *Minority Report* style of interaction and to support new kinds of game interaction.

While gaming has pushed vision-based interaction hardware and capabilities in recent years, another relatively new area that is attracting interest and motivating a good deal of research in the area is human-robot interaction. Perceiving the identity, activity, and intent of humans is

---

[1] http://www.playstation.com/
[2] http://www.xbox.com/kinect
[3] http://www.leapmotion.com/

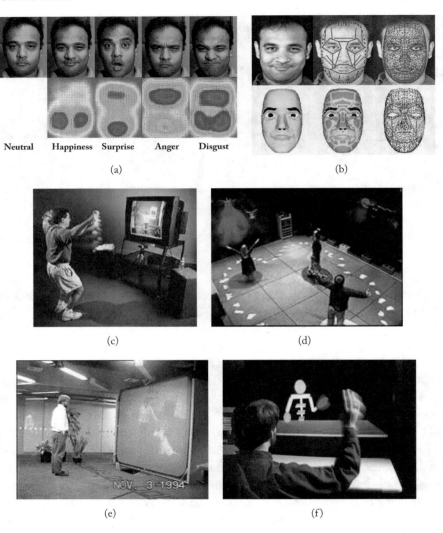

Neutral   Happiness   Surprise   Anger   Disgust

(a)

(b)

(c)

(d)

(e)

(f)

Figure 1.4: Examples of VBI research at the MIT Media Lab in the 1990s. (a) Facial expression analysis. (b) Face modeling. (c) An interactive exercise coach. (d) The KidsRoom. (e) Pfinder. (f) Head and hands based tracking and interaction.

fundamental to enabling rich, friendly interaction between robots and people in several important areas of application, including robot companions and pets (especially for children and the elderly), search and rescue robots, remote medicine robots, and entertainment robots.

There are many other areas in which advances in vision-based interaction can make a significant practical difference—in sports motion analysis, physical therapy and rehabilitation, augmented reality shopping, and remote control of various kinds, to name a few. Advances in hardware combined with progress in real-time tracking, face detection and recognition, depth sensing, feature descriptors, and machine learning-based classification has translated to a first generation of commercial success in VBI.

1.4   OPPORTUNITIES AND CHALLENGES FOR VBI

We have seen solid progress in the field of computer vision toward the goal of robust, real-time visual tracking, modeling, and recognition of humans and their activities. The recent advances in commercially viable computer vision technologies are encouraging for a field that had seen relatively little commercial success in its 50-year history. However, there are still many difficult problems to solve in order to create truly robust vision-based interaction capabilities, and to integrate them in applications that can perform effectively in the real world, not just in laboratory settings or on standard databases. For VBI applications, and especially for multimodal systems that seek to integrate visual input with other modalities, the context of the interaction is particularly important, including the visual context (lighting conditions and other environmental variables that can impact performance), the task context (what is the range of VBI tasks required in a particular scenario?), and the user context (how can prior information about the user's appearance and behavior be used to customize and improve the methods?).

Face detection and recognition methods currently perform best for frontal face views with neutral expressions under even, well-lit conditions. Significant deviations from these conditions, as well as occlusion of the face (including wearing sunglasses or new changes in facial hair), cause performance to rapidly deteriorate. Body tracking performs well using RGBD sensors when movement is restricted to a relatively small set of configurations, but problems arise when there is significant self-occlusion, a large range of motion, loose clothing, or an outdoor setting. Certain body poses (e.g., one arm raised) or repetitive gestures (e.g., waving) can be recognized effectively, but others—especially subtle gestures that can be very important in human-human interaction—are difficult in general contexts. On a higher level, the problem of correctly interpreting human intent from expression, pose, and gesture is very complex, and far from solved despite some interesting work in this direction.

The first generation of vision-based interaction technologies have focused on methods to build component technologies in specific imaging contexts—face recognition systems in biometrics scenarios, gesture recognition in living room gaming, etc. The current challenge and opportunity for the field is to develop new approaches that will scale to a broader range of scenarios and integrate effectively with other modalities and the semantics of the context at hand.

1.5   ORGANIZATION

In the following chapters, we discuss the primary components of vision-based interaction, present state-of-the-art approaches to the key detection and recognition problems, and suggest directions for exploration. Chapter 2 covers methods for detection and recognition of faces, hands, and bodies. Chapter 3 discusses both static and dynamic elements of the relevant technologies. In Chapter 4, we summarize multimodal interaction and the relationship of computer vision methods to other modalities, and Chapter 5 comments on current and future applications of VBI. We conclude with a summary and a view to the future in Chapter 6.

CHAPTER 2

Awareness: Detection and Recognition

Sensing people is the core functionality of the visual processing unit of a vision-based interaction system. The ultimate goal of human sensing is to endow computers with a capacity to fully interpret human communicative behaviors. To achieve this, the visual processing unit of a vision-based interface should address the three key tasks of *awareness*, *control*, and *feedback* depicted in Figure 1.1. We refer to these components as the awareness processor, the control processor, and the feedback processor, respectively, and we focus primarily on the first two; designing an effective feedback processor is an important human-computer interaction task that is quite application specific.

The awareness processor gathers information about the user without an explicit attempt at communication. In other words, it gathers the visual and environmental context of the user—which may be quite useful in and of itself—and prepares the system for any potential communication from the user. A vision-based interface running in the awareness mode functions as a hidden assistant, observing but not directly communicating with the user. The system may or may not act, depending on the context. The control processor, on the other hand, deals with explicit and purposive communication from the users for system controls—e.g., go/stop, put object A at place B, or hit the ball—expressing intentionality. The feedback processor provides prompt visual feedback to guide the user to perform more control actions and to confirm accomplishment of previous actions.

Even with specific control and feedback components, vision-based interaction may seem to diverge from some design principles of traditional, direct manipulation human-computer interaction, such as comprehensibility and predictability [Shneiderman *et al.*, 2010]. Yet they still share many common principles, such as seeking to provide sufficient interactive feedback about a user's accomplishments. This is important, as people constantly look for feedback to confirm the effectiveness of a conversation or communication in their daily lives. However, the expectations for interaction are expected to change as the context becomes more like human-human interaction, which is full of ambiguities and procedures to achieve disambiguation, and less like desktop work.

In this chapter, we focus our discussion on the awareness processor in a vision-based interface. In particular, we discuss technologies which enables a machine to answer the following questions [Turk, 1998]:

- Is anyone there?

- Where are they?

- Who are they?

- What are their movements?

- What are their facial expressions?

- Are their lips moving?

- What gestures they making?

Clearly, visual detection and recognition technologies are important to address these questions. However not all vision-based interfaces need to address each of these questions; the subset of questions to be addressed largely depends on the intended applications of such an interface.

2.1   WHAT TO DETECT AND RECOGNIZE?

Visual detection refers to the process of identifying and localizing certain visual phenomena or visual objects in the images and videos. For example, detecting human faces from an image has been an active research area in computer vision for several decades. In a broad sense, visual detection by itself can be viewed as a visual recognition problem. The seminal Viola-Jones face detector [Viola and Jones, 2001] takes a scanning window approach and efficiently determines if each window is a human face or not—it is just a two-class classification problem.

Visual recognition, on the other hand, is more broad, in which the goal is to perceive all different levels of visual semantics. In a recognition problem, the visual semantics of interest may be as holistic as a visual scene [Oliva and Torralba, 2001], or as fine-grained as a leaf of a plant [Belhumeur et al., 2008]. For vision-based interaction, the semantics of interest should of course be related to the human subject. For example, to interpret if there are any users present, a vision-based interface may attempt to detect human faces in the scene. If there are detected human faces, then the system will be aware that they are potential users who may be seeking more interaction.

The ultimate goal of vision-based interaction is to make machines that are aware of all the subtleties in visual communications. To be able to achieve this goal, there is a set of visual semantics or visual attributes related to the subject which needs to be effectively perceived, including

- **Presence**: Detecting the presence of the user is very important for a vision-based interface to be aware of potential interactive communications from the user. The presence of a user could be defined in different ways according to the feasible field of view of the interface. The presence of a user means the user or some body parts of a user entered the feasible field of view and was able to perform interaction at some point in time. For example, for a full-body action-based interface, such as Microsoft Kinect [Shotton *et al.*, 2011], the feasible field of view of the interface is the space where the camera of the vision-based interface can see the full human body. Similarly, for a hand gesture-based interface, such as HandVu [Kölsch, 2004], a user is present when his/her hand enters the feasible field of view.

- **Location**: Location is a very important situated context of a vision-based interface. It is a strong indicator of the user's intention. For example, if from the location of the user we detect that he/she is approaching the machine, then there is a high probability that the user wants to interact with it. The system can begin more detailed visual sensing of the user to better serve potential interactions. For a vision-based interface built into mobile phones, location sensing becomes even more important since it is possible to obtain the rich environment context related to location to better serve the needs of the user.

- **Identity**: Recognizing the identity of the users can serve two purposes. On one hand, a user profile may be leveraged to provide more personalized interaction schemes. For example, in a vision-based interface for a game console, if the system senses that a user named John Smith is in the vicinity, it may issue a proactive welcome greeting like "Hi John, do you want to play?" On the other hand, successfully recognizing the identity of the user is essential for supporting multiple user interactions as we need to simultaneously support individual demands of the different users.

- **Gesture**: Hand and body gestures are essential elements of human-human communication, which is largely complementary to verbal communication. For vision-based interaction, gesture recognition not only provides a natural means for control, but also provides subtle information about the user's mind set. For example, a user may habitually crosses his fingers or bite his fingernails when he is anxious or when he is very happy. Therefore, from gesture recognition, the vision-based interface can potentially infer the user's affective states.

- **Facial expression**: Facial expression directly relates to user emotion. Hence facial expression recognition provides valuable information in cognition of the emotion of the users [Dornaika and Raducanu, 2008]. Accurate recognition of facial expressions may allow us to not only closely follow the user's emotion, but also to provide a valuable mechanism to sense the satisfaction of the user [Picard, 1999]. This makes the vision-based interface to be adaptive to the user's emotional state. Due to the high correlation between facial expression and affect/emotion states, a majority of the research on vision-based affect computing has been devoted to facial expression recognition and analysis [Zeng *et al.*, 2009].

- **Eye gaze/attention**: Eye gaze directly relates to the attention of the users. It plays a very important role in expressing the users' needs, desire, cognitive processes, and personal emotions. For vision-based interaction, eye gaze provides valuable information about where the user's attention is focused. Hence this valuable feedback information can be leveraged to better serve the user's intention. Efficient and accurate detection of eye gaze and attention has been an active research topic for decades. A recent survey by Hansen and Ji [2010] presented a comprehensive review of recent progresses on modeling eyes and gaze.

- **Age**: Users of different age often present different behaviors when interacting with computer applications. Due to usability and privacy concerns, it may not always be feasible to ask users to provide their ages. For a vision-based interface, estimating the user's age becomes a desirable functionality. If this information is obtained in a non-invasive fashion, allowing the vision-based interface to tailor and adapt itself to the interaction behavior of the user's age group, the interface may achieve better user satisfaction.

A vision-based interface may provide detection and recognition of all or a subset of these attributes. Nevertheless, the semantics of interest for vision-based interaction can be obtained from different aspects or components of the human body such as the eyes, the face, the head, the hands, and the full body. Figure 2.1 illustrates the body parts from which the various semantics we discussed can be obtained. It also presents the expected semantic information each part of the body can provide for vision-based interaction.

Specifically, the face is the single richest visual information source for identifying awareness semantics for vision-based interaction. Therefore, the face has always been a key subject in vision-based interfaces. In particular, facial expression analysis is closely related to affective computing and emotion recognition [Jaimes and Sebe, 2005; Pantic and Rothkrantz, 2000; Picard, 1997], providing vital cues for sensing the affective states of the users. As illustrated by Ekman [2005], it is widely believed that the affective states of humans are connected to other functions such as attention, perception, memory, decision-making, and learning, but in a rather obscure way.

Gestures are tied to particular configurations of the hands or the full body. People use a wide range of gestures in daily communication, which can be as simple as finger pointing to an object or as complicated as a shrug to express that "I don't know the answer" or "I don't care about the results" [Ning *et al.*, 2006]. Meanwhile, eye gaze/attention detection and tracking not only provides advanced input in vision-based interaction, but also serves as important evidence for cognitive scientists to study human cognitive processes [Chen and Ji, 2011; Liversedge and Findlay, 2000; Mason *et al.*, 2004].

In summary, the available visual input for nonverbal communication naturally categorizes research on visual detection and recognition for human computer interaction, and it has driven the key research we describe in the following section.

2.2   REVIEW OF STATE-OF-THE-ART AND SEMINAL WORKS

In this section, we will summarize some of the seminal works in each category of the detection and recognition tasks based on the input granularity. For each category, we will briefly discuss the state-of-the-art and select one piece of seminal work to describe in detail, which is intended

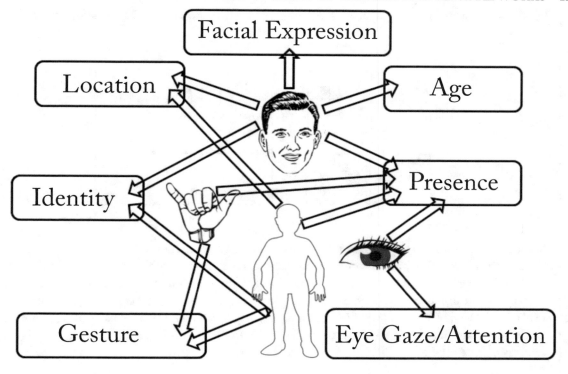

Figure 2.1: Sensing people at different granularities, i.e., eye, face, hands, and body, etc.

to suggest candidate technological components to readers who wish to improve upon existing techniques to build vision-based interfaces.

2.2.1   FACE

The face is one of the most widely studied subjects when sensing people from videos and images. In this subsection, we will discuss various aspects of facial analysis, including face detection (location and presence), face recognition (identity), facial expression recognition, and age estimation from face images.

Face Detection

Despite previous successful work on face detection [Papageorgiou *et al.*, 1998a; Rowley *et al.*, 1998; Schneiderman and Kanade, 2000; Sung and Poggio, 1998; Yang *et al.*, 2000], ever since the publication of the Viola-Jones face detector [Viola and Jones, 2001], the Boosting Cascade detector has become the predominant detection framework—the majority of subsequent research has followed the same framework. We refer the reader to Zhang and Zhang [2010] for a comprehensive summary of recent progress for research on face detection under the Boosting framework.

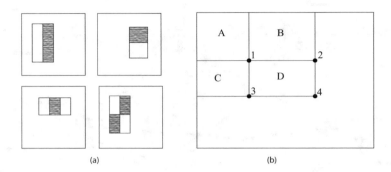

Figure 2.2: Column (a) shows several Haar-like filters. To compute the Haar feature, the sum of pixels in the black region of the box filter is subtracted from the sum of the pixels in the white region. Column (b) illustrates that if we build an integral image, then the sum of the pixel in any rectangular region can be calculated in $O(1)$ time, e.g., as shown in the image in the column (b), region $D = II(4) + II(1) - [II(2) + II(3)]$. II is the integral image, in which the pixel value at (i, j) are the sum of the pixels inside the rectangle of $[(0,0), (0, j), (i, 0), (i, j)]$ of the original image I (figures courtesy of Viola and Jones [2001]).

The effectiveness and efficiency of the Viola-Jones face detector depends on two algorithmic aspects: (1) the integral image techniques to compute Haar-like features in $O(1)$ time, as illustrated in Figure 2.2, and (2) the Cascade classifier induced from Boosting feature selection which allows early rejection in the detection process without evaluating all features, as presented in Figure 2.3. As summarized in Zhang and Zhang [2010], there have been a large number of later works improving on the original Viola-Jones face detector on different aspects. However, not many of them have proven to be significantly more powerful than the original Viola-Jones detector. OMRON, a Japanese company, has engineered one of the best (and best known) industrial quality face detectors, following the Boosting cascade framework.

Face Recognition
Face recognition is an extensively studied topic in the past couple decades [Ahonen *et al.*, 2004; Belhumeur *et al.*, 1997; Chen *et al.*, 2013; Cui *et al.*, 2013; Georghiades *et al.*, 2001; He *et al.*, 2005; Hua and Akbarzadeh, 2009; Li *et al.*, 2013; Lucey and Chen, 2006; Moghaddam *et al.*, 2000; Samaria and Harter, 1994; Takacs, 1998; Turk and Pentland, 1991b; Wiskott *et al.*, 1997; Wolf *et al.*, 2008a; Wright and Hua, 2009; Yin *et al.*, 2011]. While earlier work largely focused on applications related to biometrics and access control, where the environment is more or less controlled, recent work has been more focused on face recognition in images from unconstrained

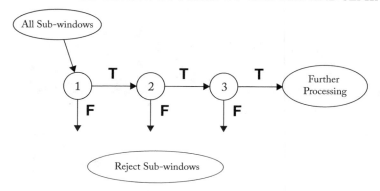

Figure 2.3: The detector takes a scanning window approach and tries to make a binary classification for each window. The cascade classifier built from AdaBoosting allows quick early rejection of a sub-window if it is unlikely to be a detection (figure courtesy of Viola and Jones [2001]).

sources, such as those images shared online on social networking sites [Hua and Akbarzadeh, 2009; Wolf *et al.*, 2008a; Wright and Hua, 2009; Yin *et al.*, 2011] and mobile human-computer interaction scenarios.

There are two common tasks in face recognition, namely *face verification* and *face identification*. For face verification, one needs to determine if a pair of face images or face image tracks[1] are from the same person or not. For face identification, the task is to recognize the identity of an input face image or a track of face images (the probe face), based on a set of labeled faces (the gallery faces). Algorithms designed for face verification can be applied to face identification by appropriately aggregating together the pairwise verification results between the probe face and each of the gallery faces. The accuracy of the face recognition system is largely determined by how robust its visual matching algorithm is to the challenging range of facial variations.

In computer vision, researchers in face recognition advocate rigorous evaluation of research progress with systematically constructed benchmark datasets. Some of the widely adopted benchmark datasets, in chronological order, include the YALE face dataset [Belhumeur *et al.*, 1997; Georghiades *et al.*, 2001], the FERET dataset [Philips *et al.*, 2000], the FRGC dataset [Phillips *et al.*, 2005], the PIE dataset [Sim *et al.*, 2003], the Multi-PIE dataset [Gross *et al.*, 2010], the Labeled Faces in the Wild (LFW) dataset [Huang *et al.*, 2007b], and the YouTube video face recognition dataset [Wolf *et al.*, 2011]. While the YALE, FERET, FRGC PIE, Multi-PIE datasets are more or less taken under controlled or semi-controlled environment, the LFW and the YouTube datasets are gathered from images and videos from the Internet, which are taken from unconstrained sources, or in other words, from "the wild."

As pointed out in Hua *et al.* [2011], it may be the case that face recognition algorithms that work best on face images from unconstrained sources may actually perform worse on face images

---

[1]We define a *face image track* as a set of face images of an individual tracked through a video segment.

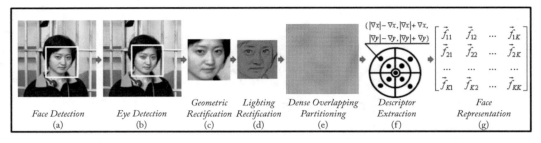

Figure 2.4: A dense visual descriptor-based representation (figure courtesy of Hua and Akbarzadeh [2009]).

from controlled environments. This is not surprising, as many modern face matching algorithms are based on statistical learning, and thus are tuned to the statistics of the target dataset. While we should always embrace methods where they are effective, it may also be desirable to have face recognition algorithms which are not heavily tuned toward the statistics of the specific target data set, because such an algorithm may not generalize well across different datasets. Such a mismatch of data statistics between training and testing may be partly relieved by domain transfer learning methods [Cao and Wipf, 2013]. However, real applications may require that the face recognition algorithm be plug-and-play without requiring any additional training.

Hua and Akbarzadeh [2009] proposed a robust elastic and partial matching algorithm for face recognition, which has demonstrated good recognition performance on face recognition benchmarks from both unconstrained environments, such as the LFW dataset [Huang *et al.*, 2007b], and constraint environments, such as the PIE [Sim *et al.*, 2003] dataset and the YALE face dataset [Belhumeur *et al.*, 1997; Georghiades *et al.*, 2001]. This matching algorithm does not rely on heavy machine learning and is designed to be robust against pose variations and partial occlusions, which are the reasons that it achieves good recognition accuracy while retaining a good generalization capability across different datasets.

The computational process of the numerical representation of the face image in [Hua and Akbarzadeh, 2009] is shown in Figure 2.4. It takes a dense descriptor-based representation, where local image descriptors are extracted from densely sampled image patches of the geometric and photometric rectified face images. Therefore the final face representation is the set of all descriptors arranged in a two-dimensional array, as illustrated in Figure 2.4 (g). With this face representation, a robust elastic and partial matching metric is designed for calculating the distance from a pair of face images, which is illustrated in Figure 2.5. In essence, the distance defined from this matching process can be regarded as a spatial position constrained generalized Hausdorff distance [Takacs, 1998] in the descriptor space. The physical interpretation of such a distance is indeed quite meaningful; e.g., if the distance is d, it means that α percent of the descriptors in one face image found a matched descriptor in the local spatial neighborhood in the other face image with distance less than d. Hua and Akbarzadeh [2009] reveal that $\alpha = 20$ usually achieves

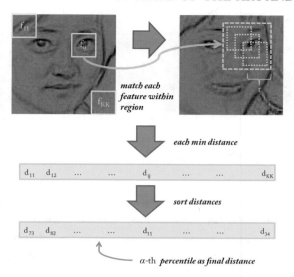

Figure 2.5: A robust distance measure by elastic and partial matching: to match two faces, each local descriptor in one face image is matched with local descriptors in a neighborhood in the other face image. The minimal match distance is recorded for each descriptor and put in an array. The minimum distance array is sorted in the end with the α-th percentile distance picked up as the matching distance of the two faces (figure courtesy of Hua and Akbarzadeh [2009]).

the optimal performance. This is somewhat surprising as it implies that the match of two face images largely relies on only 20% of the face regions.

This elastic partial matching metric does not rely on heavy-duty machine learning, and it has been proven to generalize well across different face recognition benchmarks. Hence it can often be employed as a plug-and-play module. Nevertheless, the matching process can be computationally expensive, for which Wright and Hua [2009] proposed a joint spatial-feature visual vocabulary-based representation of faces, where the elastic matching is made implicit in the matching process. This new representation allows for efficient inverted file indexing of gallery face images. Hence it is another option for when speed is an issue, especially when matching against a large number of gallery faces.

Recently, there have been significant research advances in enhancing face verification accuracy in real-world images, such as Chen *et al.* [2013]; Cui *et al.* [2013]; Li *et al.* [2013], which are among the best performing algorithms on the LFW dataset to date. They use various training protocols depending on whether or not external data is leveraged for alignment, feature extraction, or training the recognition algorithm. All these recent advancements suggest that it is beneficial

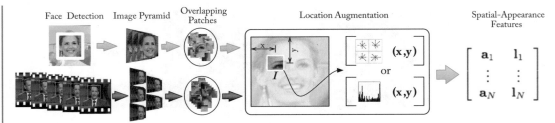

Figure 2.6: The spatial-appearance feature extraction pipeline in the PEM method.

to (1) exploit very high dimensional visual features and (2) fuse several feature types to achieve the level of invariance for robust face verification under uncontrolled settings.

In particular, Li *et al.* [2013] presented a probabilistic elastic matching (PEM) method for pose invariant face verification, which provided a unified framework for both image- and video-based face verification. This system achieves robustness to pose variations, an ability to generalize with limited training data, and state-of-the-art results on the most restricted protocol on the LFW Dataset and the YouTube Video Face Dataset. In the following, we present the details of each technical component in this algorithm.

Spatial-appearance Feature Extraction. For image-based face verification, the PEM method initially represents each face image as a bag of spatial-appearance features. As shown in Figure 2.6, for each face image $\mathcal{F}$, it first builds a three-layer Gaussian image pyramid. It then densely extracts overlapping image patches from each level of the image pyramid. The set of all N patches extracted from face image $\mathcal{F}$ is denoted as $\mathcal{P} = \{p_i\}_{i=1}^N$. Next, it extracts an appearance feature from each image patch p_i, denoted as $\mathbf{a}_{p_i}$. Finally, it augments the appearance feature of each patch p_i with its coordinates $\mathbf{l}_{p_i} = [x\ y]^T$ as its spatial feature. As a result, the final feature representation for patch p_i is a spatial-appearance feature $\mathbf{f}_{p_i} = [\mathbf{a}_{p_i}^T, \mathbf{l}_{p_i}^T]^T$. The final representation for face image $\mathcal{F}$ is hence an ensemble of these spatial-appearance features, i.e., $\mathbf{f}_{\mathcal{F}} = \{\mathbf{f}_{p_i}\}_{i=1}^N$.

In video-based face verification, the task is to verify if two tracks of faces are from the same person or not (assuming constant identity throughout each track of faces). The PEM method adopts the same bag of spatial-appearance feature representation for a track of faces by repeating the feature extraction pipeline in Figure 2.6 on each face image in the track. The features extracted from the face images from a single track are joined together to form a larger set of spatial-appearance features, which serve as the final representation of a face track. As a result, we take the same kind of feature representation for both image-based and video-based face verification. Therefore, the probabilistic elastic matching method introduced in the following section will apply to both image- and video-based face verification.

Probabilistic Elastic Matching. The exact steps of the probabilistic elastic matching method are illustrated in Figure 2.7. It starts by building a Gaussian Mixture Model (GMM) from all the

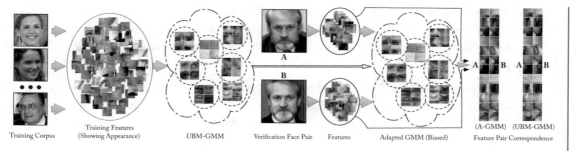

Training Corpus | Training Features (Showing Appearance) | UBM-GMM | Verification Face Pair | Features | Adapted GMM (Biased) | (A-GMM) (UBM-GMM) Feature Pair Correspondence

Figure 2.7: The PEM pipeline to build feature pair correspondence.

spatial-appearance features extracted from face images in the training set. Following the terminology from the speech recognition community [Hasan and Hansen, 2011], such a GMM is called a Universal Background Model (UBM) or UBM-GMM.

Given a face/face track pair, both of which are represented as a bag of spatial-appearance features, for each Gaussian component in the UBM-GMM, it looks for a pair of features (one from each of the face images/tracks) that induce the highest probability on it. Such a pair of features is named a *corresponding feature pair*. The absolute difference vectors of all these corresponding feature pairs are concatenated together to form a long vector, which is subsequently fed into an SVM classifier for prediction.

An additional improvement is to conduct a joint Bayesian adaptation step to adapt the UBM-GMM to the union of the spatial-appearance features from both face images/tracks, constrained *a priori* by the parameters of the original UBM-GMM, to form a new GMM (A-GMM). Then the A-GMM can be used instead of the UBM-GMM to build the corresponding feature pairs. Therefore, the proposed approach using UBM-GMM to build the corresponding feature pair is named *probabilistic elastic matching* (PEM), and the approach using A-GMM to build the corresponding feature pair is named *adaptive probabilistic elastic matching* (APEM).

The detailed description of the key steps of the PEM method including the training of the UBM-GMM, the invariant matching scheme, and the joint Bayesian adaptation algorithm for the APEM are presented below:

1. **Training UBM-GMM.** As discussed before, GMM as UBM is widely used in the area of speech recognition [Hasan and Hansen, 2011]. In the PEM method, to balance the impact of the appearance and spatial location, the UBM is confined to be a GMM with spherical Gaussian components, i.e.,

$$P(\mathbf{f}|\Theta) = \sum_{k=1}^{K} \omega_k \mathcal{G}(\mathbf{f}|\vec{\mu}_k, \sigma_k^2 \mathbf{I}), \qquad (2.1)$$

where $\Theta = (\omega_1, \vec{\mu}_1, \sigma_1, \ldots, \omega_K, \vec{\mu}_K, \sigma_K)$; K is the number of Gaussian mixture components; $\mathbf{I}$ is an identity matrix; ω_k is the mixture weight of the k-th Gaussian component; $\mathcal{G}(\mu_k, \sigma_k^2 \mathbf{I})$ is a spherical Gaussian with mean μ_k and variance $\sigma_k^2 \mathbf{I}$, and $\mathbf{f}$ is an m-dimensional spatial-appearance feature vector, i.e., $\mathbf{f} = [\mathbf{a}^T \ \mathbf{l}^T]^T$.

To fit such a UBM-GMM over the training feature set $\chi = \{\mathbf{f}_1, \mathbf{f}_2, \ldots, \mathbf{f}_M\}$, we resort to the Expectation-Maximization (EM) algorithm to obtain an estimate of the parameters of the GMM by maximizing the likelihood $\mathcal{L}$ of the training features χ, formally,

$$\Theta^* \quad = \quad \arg\max_{\Theta} \mathcal{L}(\chi|\Theta) \tag{2.2}$$

The EM algorithm consists of the **E**-step which computes the expected log-likelihood and the **M**-step which updates parameters to maximize this expected log-likelihood [Gauvain and Lee, 1994]. Specifically, in the **E**-step, the following sufficient statistics are calculated, i.e.,

$$n_k = \sum_{i=1}^{M} P(k|\mathbf{f}_i), \tag{2.3}$$

$$E_k(\mathbf{f}) = \frac{1}{n_k} \sum_{i=1}^{M} P(k|\mathbf{f}_i)\mathbf{f}_i, \tag{2.4}$$

$$E_k(\mathbf{f}^T\mathbf{f}) = \frac{1}{n_k} \sum_{i=1}^{M} P(k|\mathbf{f}_i)\mathbf{f}_i^T\mathbf{f}_i, \tag{2.5}$$

where $P(k|\mathbf{f}_i)$ is defined as

$$P(k|\mathbf{f}_i) = \frac{\omega_k \mathcal{G}(\mathbf{f}_i|\mu_k, \sigma_k^2\mathbf{I})}{\sum_{k'=1}^{K} \omega_{k'} \mathcal{G}(\mathbf{f}_i|\mu_{k'}, \sigma_{k'}^2\mathbf{I})} \tag{2.6}$$

which is the posterior probability that the k-th Gaussian component generated feature $\mathbf{f}_i$. In the **M**-step, the parameter set Θ is updated as

$$\hat{\omega}_k \quad = \quad \frac{n_k}{M}, \tag{2.7}$$

$$\hat{\mu}_k \quad = \quad E_k(\mathbf{f}), \tag{2.8}$$

$$\hat{\sigma}_k^2 \quad = \quad \frac{1}{m}(E_k(\mathbf{f}^T\mathbf{f}) - \hat{\mu}_k^T\hat{\mu}_k). \tag{2.9}$$

These two steps are iterated until convergence, at which time we obtain the UBM-GMM. Note that variances along different dimensions are indeed taken into consideration through Equation 2.9.

With the location-augmented feature, it is a well-recognized problem that the spatial constraint from the augmented l can be too weak to have an impact if treated in a straightforward manner. This is because the dimension m_a of the appearance feature a can be considerably larger in practice than the dimension of the location feature l, which is $m_l = 2$ in our experiments.

Here we demonstrate that confining each mixture component in the GMM to be a spherical Gaussian can handle this issue, as it helps establish a balance between the spatial and appearance constraints. Take the k-th Gaussian component $P(\mathbf{f}|\omega_k, \mu_k, \sigma_k^2 \mathbf{I})$ as an example, the probability feature $\mathbf{f}$ over it is

$$\mathcal{G}(\mathbf{f}|\vec{\mu}_k, \sigma_k^2 \mathbf{I}) \propto e^{-\frac{\|\mathbf{a}-\vec{\mu}_k^a\|^2}{2\sigma_k^2}} e^{-\frac{\|\mathbf{l}-\vec{\mu}_k^l\|^2}{2\sigma_k^2}}, \qquad (2.10)$$

where $\vec{\mu}_k^a$ and $\vec{\mu}_k^l$ are the appearance and location parts of $\vec{\mu}_k$, such that $\vec{\mu}_k = [\vec{\mu}_k^{aT}, \vec{\mu}_k^{lT}]^T$. As shown in Equation 2.10, the spherical Gaussian on the spatial-appearance model can be regarded as the product of two equal variance Gaussian distributions over two Euclidean distances produced by the appearance and location, respectively. As long as the ranges of the two Euclidean distances are matched, the influence of these two Gaussians will be balanced. This can be easily achieved by normalizing the appearance and the location part of the spatial-appearance feature in an appropriate way, such as scaling $\mathbf{a}$ to be a unit vector and keeping every element of l has a value between 0 and 1.

As illustrated in Figure 2.8, without confining the mixture components to be spherical Gaussians, the spatial constraint introduced from l is so weak that the spatial spanning of Gaussian components are highly overlapping, which does not help build correct feature correspondences in the invariant matching stage. In contrast, the spatial variances of spherical Gaussian components are more localized, which could tolerate pose variations more appropriately.

Note that if the UBM-GMM uses normal Gaussian components, one cannot address this issue by scaling $\mathbf{a}$. This can be observed by checking the equations in the EM algorithm: if $\mathbf{a}$ is scaled, the corresponding means and covariances will be scaled proportionally. Then the probability of $\mathbf{f}$ over each of the Gaussian components will be scaled in the same way. As a result, $P(k|\mathbf{f}_i)$ is unchanged (Equation 2.6), which means the EM estimates will undesirably remain the same—it only scales the mean and variance estimates. This is unable to help balance the influence of the appearance and the location.

2. **Invariant Matching.** After the K-components UBM-GMM trained over a set of m-dimensional spatial-appearance features are obtained, we exploit these to form an elastic matching scheme in the form of a $D = m \times K$ dimensional difference vector for a pair of face images/tracks.

 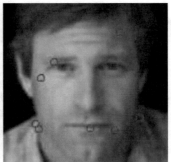

(a) UBM - normal Gaussians   (b) UBM - spherical Gaussians

Figure 2.8: Spatial distribution of 10 selected Gaussian components in the UBM over a face. Each red ellipse (or circle) stands for a Gaussian component. The center and span show mean and variance of the spatial part of the Gaussian component.

Formally, a face/face track $\mathcal{F}$ is presented as a bag of spatial-appearance features $\mathbf{f}_{\mathcal{F}} = \{\mathbf{f}_1, \mathbf{f}_2, \ldots, \mathbf{f}_N\}$. In the first step, each Gaussian component $(\omega_k, \mathcal{G}_k(\vec{\mu}_k, \sigma_k^2 \mathcal{I}))$ contributes one feature $f_{g_k(\mathcal{F})}$ from $\mathbf{f}_{\mathcal{F}}$, such that

$$g_k(\mathcal{F}) = \arg \max_i \omega_k \mathcal{G}(\mathbf{f}_i | \vec{\mu}_k, \sigma_k^2 \mathbf{I}). \tag{2.11}$$

The face/face track $\mathcal{F}$ is then represented as a sequence of K m-dimensional features, i.e., $[\mathbf{f}_{g_1} \mathbf{f}_{g_2} \ldots \mathbf{f}_{g_K}]$. After this stage, given the i-th faces/face tracks pair ($\mathcal{F}$ and $\mathcal{F}'$), the difference vector is a concatenated vector, i.e.,

$$\mathbf{d}_i = [\Delta \mathbf{a}_{g_1} \Delta \mathbf{a}_{g_2} \ldots \Delta \mathbf{a}_{g_K}]^T, \tag{2.12}$$

where $\Delta \mathbf{a}_{g_k} = |\mathbf{a}_{g_k(\mathcal{F})} - \mathbf{a}_{g_k(\mathcal{F}')}|^T$, which serves as the final matching feature vector of a pair of faces/face tracks for face verification. Note that this final representation is focused on the appearance differences, since the spatial component is already taken into consideration when we build the corresponding feature pairs. The way we build correspondence from the spatial-appearance GMM model is motivated by and related to max pooling and the lateral inhibition mechanism in receptive fields; both have been proven to be beneficial when building visual representations.

A kernel SVM classifier, i.e.,

$$f(\mathbf{d}) = \sum_{i=1}^{v} \alpha_i k(\mathbf{d}_i, \mathbf{d}) + b, \tag{2.13}$$

is then trained over C training difference vectors $\{\mathbf{d}_1, \mathbf{d}_2, \ldots, \mathbf{d}_C\}$ with the Gaussian Radial Basis Function (RBF) kernel, i.e.,

$$k(\mathbf{d}_i, \mathbf{d}_j) = exp(-\gamma||\mathbf{d}_i - \mathbf{d}_j||^2), \gamma > 0, \tag{2.14}$$

where $i, j = 1, \ldots, C$. Given the difference vector $\mathbf{d}_t$ of a testing face/face track pair, the SVM predicts its label. The LibSVM [Chang and Lin, 2011] is leveraged to train the SVM classifier. The matching algorithm presented in this section is called *probabilistic elastic matching* (PEM).

3. **Joint Bayesian Model Adaptation.** Prior work applying GMMs with Bayesian adaptation to visual recognition [Dixit *et al.*, 2011; Zhou *et al.*, 2009] has operated either at the class level or at the image level. To make the matching process adaptive to each face/face track pair, a joint Bayesian adaptation on the union of the bag of spatial-appearance features from the faces/face tracks pair is proposed. In the joint adaptation process, the parameters of the UBM-GMM build the prior distribution for the parameters of the jointly adapted GMM under a Bayesian maximum a posteriori (MAP) framework.

For ease of presentation, the UBM parameter set is denoted as Θ_b and parameter set of the GMM after joint adaptation is denoted as Θ_p, where $\Theta_x = \{\omega_{x_1}, \vec{\mu}_{x_1}, \sigma_{x_1}, \ldots, \omega_{x_K}, \vec{\mu}_{x_K}, \sigma_{x_K}\}$, $x = \{b, p\}$. Given a face/face track pair $\mathcal{Q}$ and $\mathcal{S}$, the adaptive GMM is trained over the joint feature set $\chi_p = \{\mathbf{f}_1, \mathbf{f}_2, \ldots, \mathbf{f}_P\}$ which is the union of feature sets of $\mathcal{Q}$ and $\mathcal{S}$ as χ_q and χ_s, where $|\chi_p| = |\chi_q| + |\chi_s|$. Upon χ_p a MAP estimate for Θ_p can be obtained by maximizing the log-likelihood $\mathcal{L}(\Theta_p)$, i.e.,

$$\mathcal{L}(\Theta_p) = ln P(\chi_p|\Theta_p) + ln P(\Theta_p|\Theta_b). \tag{2.15}$$

The conjugate prior distribution of Θ_p is composed from the UBM-GMM parameter Θ_b [Dixit *et al.*, 2011; Gauvain and Lee, 1994; Zhou *et al.*, 2009], i.e.,

$$(\omega_{p_1}, \ldots, \omega_{p_K}) \quad \sim \quad Dir(T\omega_{b_1}, \ldots, T\omega_{b_K}), \tag{2.16}$$
$$\mu_{p_k} \quad \sim \quad \mathcal{N}(\vec{\mu}_{b_k}, \sigma_{b_k}^2/\gamma). \tag{2.17}$$

The prior distribution over the mixture weights is a Dirichlet distribution. The parameter T can be interpreted as the count of features introduced by the UBM-GMM. The prior distribution for mean μ_{p_k} is a spherical Gaussian distribution with variance smoothed by parameter γ. We can also use a Normal-Wishart distribution over the variance as in [Dixit *et al.*, 2011; Gauvain and Lee, 1994]. However, in order to stabilize the adapted GMM, we confined the adapted variance to be the same as that of the UBM-GMM, i.e, $\sigma_{p_k}^2 = \sigma_{b_k}^2$.

With these priors, the parameters of the adapted GMM can be estimated by a Bayesian EM algorithm [Dixit *et al.*, 2011; Gauvain and Lee, 1994; Zhou *et al.*, 2009], i.e., in the

(a) Feature correspondences built through UBM-GMM

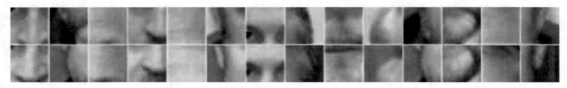

(b) Feature correspondences built through A-GMM

Figure 2.9: In both figures, the top row comprises local patches from face A shown in Figure 2.7, while the bottom row patches are from face B. Each column shows a pair of features captured by one Gaussian component in the GMM.

E-step, the following statistics are computed:

$$n_k = \sum_{i=1}^{P} P(k|\mathbf{f}_i), \tag{2.18}$$

$$E_k(\mathbf{f}) = \frac{1}{n_k} \sum_{i=1}^{P} P(k|\mathbf{f}_i)\mathbf{f}_i, \tag{2.19}$$

where

$$P(k|\mathbf{f}_i) = \frac{\omega_{p_k} \mathcal{G}(\mathbf{f}_i|\chi_{p_k}, {}^2_{p_k})}{\sum_{k'=1}^{K} \omega_{p_{k'}} \mathcal{G}(\mathbf{f}_i|\chi_{p_{k'}}, {}^2_{p_{k'}})}, \tag{2.20}$$

and in **M**-step, each parameter in the parameter set $_p$ is updated according to

$$\hat{\omega}_{p_k} = \frac{n_k}{N} + (1 \quad)\omega_{b_k}, \tag{2.21}$$

$$\hat{\chi}_{p_k} = \sigma_k E_k(\mathbf{f}) + (1 \quad \sigma_k)\vec{\chi}_{b_k}, \tag{2.22}$$

where

$$= N/(N + T), \sigma_k = n_k/(n_k +). \tag{2.23}$$

After the adapted GMM is obtained, given a pair of faces/face tracks, the APEM method is leveraged to build the difference vector for invariant matching. It can be observed that A-GMM improves some feature correspondences as shown in Figure 2.9, such as shown in the 10th and the last column.

Multiple Feature Fusion. In visual recognition, fusing multiple types of visual features often proved to be beneficial in driving the recognition accuracy up [Chen *et al.*, 2012; Pinto *et al.*, 2009]. The PEM/APEM method can also benefit from such feature fusion by using a linear SVM to aggregate the verification score from multiple types of features.

To post-fuse multiple features, the proposed pipeline can run over all face/face track pairs using D types of different local features to obtain D confidence scores for each face/face track pair p_i as a score vector

$$\mathbf{s}_i = [s_{i_1} \; s_{i_2} \; \ldots s_{i_D}], \tag{2.24}$$

where s_{i_d} denotes the score assigned by the classifier using the d-th type of feature. Over all C training score vectors $\{\mathbf{s}_1, \mathbf{s}_2, \ldots, \mathbf{s}_C\}$ and their labels, we train a linear SVM classifier to predict the label for a testing score vector $\mathbf{s}_t$ of a face/face track pair. Such a simple scheme proved to be very effective in our experiments. We note here that more advanced methods such as multiple kernel learning (MKL) similar to what has been adopted in Pinto *et al.* [2009] can also be adopted, but no performance difference is observed when compared with this simple fusion scheme with a linear SVM.

Horizontally flip image Considering the fact that human faces are symmetric in general, we generate a horizontally flipped version of every image in the dataset. As the proposed framework could handle faces and face tracks in a unified representation, a single face image under this setting will be regarded as a two-frame pair from symmetric viewpoints. Unlike previous work flipping the face image horizontally in a similar way [Simonyan *et al.*, 2013], which needed to repeat the same pipeline over the four possible combinations between flipped and original faces and take the average distance as the measurement, PEP-representation is more suitable in utilizing the flipped face by simply replacing the occluded facial parts with the ones from the flipped faces. In other words, we simply add the descriptors from the flipped image to the descriptor set of the face, which can help to build feature correspondences in the presence of occluded facial parts.

Experimental Evaluation. To demonstrate the efficacy of the PEM/APEM methods, we present extensive experimental results over two challenging datasets, Labeled Face in the Wild (LFW) [Huang *et al.*, 2008] and the YouTube Faces Database [Wolf *et al.*, 2011].

1. **Labeled Faces in the Wild.** The Labeled Faces in the Wild (LFW) [Huang *et al.*, 2008] dataset is designed to address the unconstrained face verification problem. This challenging dataset contains more than 13,000 images from 5,749 people. In general there are two training methods over LFW: *image-restricted* method and *image-unrestricted* method. By design, the *image-restricted* paradigm does not allow experimenters to use the name of a person to infer two face images are matched or non-matched, while in the *image-unrestricted* paradigm experimenters may form as many matched or non-matched face pairs as desired for training. Over LFW, researchers are expected to explicitly state the training method they used and report performance over 10-fold cross-validation. In this experiment, the

most restricted protocol is followed, in which detected faces are aligned with the funneling method [Huang *et al.*, 2007a].

(a) **Baseline Algorithm.** To better investigate the PEM/APEM approach to pose variant face verification, we compare with a baseline algorithm that shows how well a trivial location-based feature pair matching scheme performs. The baseline algorithm provides a basis of comparison to evaluate the effectiveness of building feature pair correspondences bridged by UBM-GMM or adapted GMM. Formally, $\mathcal{F}$ and $\mathcal{F}'$ are representations of two faces, both have N features, i.e., $\mathcal{F} = \{\mathbf{f}_1 \ldots \mathbf{f}_N\}$ and $\mathcal{F}' = \{\mathbf{f}'_1 \ldots \mathbf{f}'_N\}$, where $\mathbf{f}_n$ and $\mathbf{f}'_n$ are two spatial-appearance feature from the n-th local patch at the same location. Then the concatenated difference vector between faces $\mathcal{F}$ and $\mathcal{F}'$ is $d(\mathcal{F}, \mathcal{F}') = [|\mathbf{f}_1 - \mathbf{f}'_1|^T \ldots |\mathbf{f}_N - \mathbf{f}'_N|^T]^T$. Then an SVM classifier is trained over the training difference vectors to predict if a testing face/face track pair is matched.

(b) **Settings.** In the experiments, images are center-cropped to 150x150 pixels before feature extraction. As shown in Figure 2.6, SIFT and LBP features are extracted over each scale for a 3-scale Gaussian image pyramid with scaling factor 0.9. SIFT features are extracted from patches from an 8x8 sliding window with 2-pixel spacing, and LBP features[2] are extracted from a 32x32 sliding window with 2-pixel spacing. After that, the appearance feature is augmented by the coordinates of the patch center to build the spatial-appearance feature vector. Over all training features, we trained a UBM-GMM of 1,024 spherical Gaussian components for PEM.

For APEM, given a pair of face images, all features in the joint feature set are utilized for joint adaptation. After calculating matching difference vectors, an SVM classifier was trained using RBF kernel for classification. The standard 10-fold cross-validation over View 2 is carried out to report our performance, and the View 1 dataset is not used.

(c) **Results.** As shown in Table 2.1 and Figure 2.10, the PEM/APEM methods achieved comparable results to the state-of-the-art (i.e., Simonyan *et al.* [2013]), and outperformed other previous work by a considerable margin. Its effectiveness in terms of invariant matching can be demonstrated by comparing with the baseline. We also observed that joint Bayesian adaptation and multiple features fusion bring consistent improvements. Furthermore, our approach on unaligned faces [Huang *et al.*, 2008], which are the outputs of the Viola-Jones face detector, even outperformed previous methods with faces aligned by the funneling method.

2. **YouTube Faces Dataset.** The PEM/APEM methods provide a general framework which can handle both image- and video-based face verification without modification. Wolf *et al.*

---

[2] The LBP feature is constructed in a part-based scheme by partitioning each window uniformly into 16 8x8 cells and concatenating 16 58-dimensional uniform LBP histogram [Vedaldi and Fulkerson, 2010] calculated in each cell to form the 928-dimensional LBP feature.

Table 2.1: Performance comparison on the most restricted LFW

Algorithm	Accuracy ± Error(%)
Nowak [Nowak and Jurie, 2007]	73.93 ± 0.49
Hybrid descriptor-based [Wolf *et al.*, 2008b]	78.47 ± 0.51
V1/MKL [Pinto *et al.*, 2009]	79.35 ± 0.55
Fisher vector faces [Simonyan *et al.*, 2013]	87.47 ± 1.49
Baseline (fusion, setting as in [Li *et al.*, 2013])	77.30 ± 1.59
APEM (fusion, setting as in [Li *et al.*, 2013])	84.08 ± 1.20
PEM (LBP)	83.78 ± 1.65
PEM (SIFT)	84.03 ± 1.05
PEM (fusion)	85.57 ± 0.73
APEM (LBP)	84.63 ± 1.39
APEM (SIFT)	84.37 ± 0.74
APEM (fusion)	**86.10 ± 1.09**
PEM (SIFT, unaligned)	83.05 ± 1.19

[2011] published the YouTube Faces Dataset (YTFaces) for studying the problem of unconstrained face recognition in videos. The dataset contains 3,425 videos of 1,595 different people. On average, a face track from a video clip consists of 181.3 frames of faces. Faces are detected by the Viola-Jones detector and aligned by fixing the coordinates of automatically detected facial feature points [Wolf *et al.*, 2011]. Protocols are similar to LFW, for the same purpose, and the experiments are conducted under the restricted video face verification paradigm. To date, the state-of-art performance is published by the authors using Matched Background Similarity (MBGS) algorithm with LBP feature.

(a) **Settings.** In the video faces experiments, each image frame is center-cropped to 100×100 before feature extraction. Then features are extracted in the same way for each frame, as described in the experiments on the LFW dataset. For each video, for efficiency, we randomly sampled 10 frames as the face track. In the stage of joint Bayesian adaptation, to ease the computational intensity, 10% descriptors are sampled randomly from each face track to be combined into the joint descriptor set.

(b) **Results.** As shown in Table 2.2 and Figure 2.11, the PEM/APEM methods outperformed the state-of-the-art algorithms by a significant margin. Looking at the ROC curves, it is especially encouraging to observe that the PEM/APEM methods significantly outperformed previous methods in the low false positive region. This is desirable

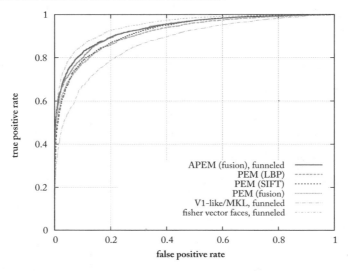

Figure 2.10: Performance comparison on the most restricted LFW.

Table 2.2: Performance comparison over YouTube Faces

Algorithm	Accuracy $\pm$ Error(%)
MBGS [Wolf *et al.*, 2011]	76.4 $\pm$ 1.8
MBGS+SVM- [Wolf and Levy, 2013]	78.9 $\pm$ 1.9
STFRD+PMML [Zhen *et al.*, 2013]	79.5 $\pm$ 2.5
VSOF+OSS(Adaboost) [Mendez-Vazquez *et al.*, 2013]	79.7 $\pm$ 1.8
PEM (LBP)	79.62 $\pm$ 1.71
PEM (SIFT)	79.78 $\pm$ 1.98
PEM (fusion)	80.60 $\pm$ 1.80
APEM (LBP)	79.82 $\pm$ 1.65
APEM (SIFT)	80.26 $\pm$ 1.96
APEM (fusion)	**81.36 $\pm$ 1.98**

as most practical applications would require that the verification algorithms operate with a low false positive rate.

We note that Cui *et al.* [2013] and Chen *et al.* [2013] achieved remarkable face verification accuracy on the LFW dataset with less restricted evaluation protocols, where external data has been

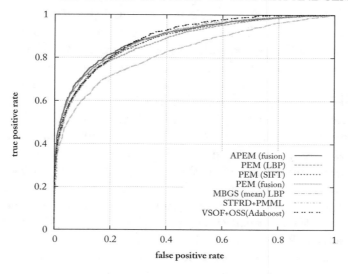

Figure 2.11: Performance comparison over YouTube Faces.

exploited for either alignment or training the recognition model. We refer interested readers to the corresponding papers for more details. In addition, there has been a tremendous amount of interest on video face recognition, where either the query face or the gallery faces or both are presented in the form of video clips. The publication of the YouTube Video Face dataset [Wolf *et al.*, 2011] has facilitated several recent publications in this area [Li *et al.*, 2013; Mendez-Vazquez *et al.*, 2013; Wolf and Levy, 2013; Zhen *et al.*, 2013], including the PEM/APEM methods.

Facial Expression Recognition

Largely due to the importance of the face in human emotion expression and perception, most vision-based affect recognition studies have been devoted to facial expression recognition and analysis. Facial expressions are the variants of facial appearances induced by a person's internal affective states, such as mood or emotion. According to Zeng *et al.* [2009], there are mainly two different approaches for facial expression recognition. The first approach attempts to recognize an expression directly from the visual images and videos [Zhang *et al.*, 1998], i.e., recognizing the facial expression directly from low-level image features. The second approach initially recognizes an intermediate layer of semantics related to facial muscle action. This is often achieved by using the representation defined in the Facial Action Coding System (FACS) proposed by Ekman and Friesen [1978]. FACS is an anatomically based system, corresponding to the underlying facial muscles, and is capable of measuring all visually discernible facial movements in terms of atomic facial actions called Action Units (AUs). The facial AUs, as a relatively objective description of facial signals, can further be mapped to the corresponding expression categories according to high-level mapping rules such as the Emotional FACS (EMFACS) or the FACS Affect Interpretation Database (FACSAID).[3] We refer the reader to De la Torre and Cohn [2011] for general background knowledge about facial expression recognition technologies.

State-of-the-art methods for facial expression analysis often employ modern pattern recognition technologies and apply them to 2D spatiotemporal features to fulfill the recognition task. The facial features can be either geometric features [Chang et al., 2006; Valstar et al., 2007], or appearance features [Anderson and McOwan, 2006; Chang et al., 2006; Guo and Dyer, 2005; Litman and Forbes-Riley, 2004; Valstar et al., 2004; Whitehill and Omlin, 2006]. For example, commonly adopted geometric features include the shapes of the facial components [Chang et al., 2006], or the locations of salient facial points [Valstar et al., 2007]. Typical example appearance features include Gabor wavelets [Guo and Dyer, 2005; Litman and Forbes-Riley, 2004], Haar features [Whitehill and Omlin, 2006], holistic spatial ratio face template [Anderson and McOwan, 2006], temporal templates using motion history image [Valstar et al., 2004], or manifold subspace of aligned face appearances [Chang et al., 2006].

Not surprisingly, several previous studies have demonstrated that the geometric and appearance features are complementary to each other [Pantic and Bartlett, 2007; Zhang et al., 1998]. Therefore, combining them together is often beneficial to improve recognition. For example, Tian et al. [2005] proposed to use a combination of facial component shapes and transient features such as crows-feet wrinkles and nasal-labial furrows for facial expression recognition. The active appearance model (AAM) [Cootes et al., 2001] has been adopted by Lucey et al. [2007] to simultaneously capture the characteristics of facial appearance and the shape of facial expression. Zhang and Ji [2005] used 26 facial points around the eyes, eyebrows, and mouth and combined these with the transient features proposed in Tian et al. [2005], which dynamically aggregates visual evidences over time to recognize the facial expression at the current time instant. Tong et al. [2007] adopted a dynamic Bayesian network (DBN) to model the dynamic and semantic relationships among the different facial action units. They demonstrated that the DBN-based joint recognition methods are more robust than those methods that individually recognize each facial action unit. The more accurate recognition of the facial action units can directly lead to more accurate facial expression recognition.

For a vision-based interface, it is important to recognize spontaneous facial expression; posed (and often exaggerated) expressions are generally not of interest, and a frontal view constraint is not practical. The techniques we have reviewed so far are largely focused on 2D features and 2D processing, which implies that they can only be applied when the head motion is within a small range. A promising path toward view independent facial expression recognition is to leverage 3D facial modeling [Cohen et al., 2003; Cohn et al., 2004; Sebe et al., 2004; Wen and Huang, 2003] and 3D expression data sets [Chang et al., 2005; Wang et al., 2006a; Yin et al., 2006]. Specifically, Cohen et al. [2003]; Sebe et al. [2004]; Wen and Huang [2003] benefited from the features extracted from a 3D face tracker proposed by Tao and Huang [1999], namely

---

[3]http://face-and-emotion.com/dataface/general/homepage.jsp

the Piecewise Bezier Volume Deformation Tracker. The system of Cohn et al. [2004] exploited a cylindrical head model [Yeasin et al., 2006]. The 3D facial expression database released by Yin et al. [2006] is considered to be the first such effort to make such a dataset publicly available to the research community.

In an orthogonal direction, just as with research on general visual recognition, state-of-the-art facial expression recognition systems have benefited greatly from statistical machine learning. A notable recent work is presented by Nicolaou et al. [2011], where an output-associative relevance vector machine (OA-RVM) regression method is proposed for dimensional and continuous emotion prediction. In Nicolaou et al. [2011], the authors focused on two latent dimensions—the *valence* dimension (V), which represents how positive or negative an emotional state is, and the arousal dimension (A), which indicates the engagement level (from apathetic to excited) of an emotional state. For continuous emotion prediction, an output-associative model can effectively model the temporal and spatial dependencies between the output vectors, the repeating output patterns, and input-output associations. Hence it leads to a more accurate prediction of continuous emotion states. We refer the reader to Nicolaou et al. [2011] for details of the OA-RVM method.

Valstar et al. [2012] presents a comprehensive summary of state-of-the-art facial expression recognition algorithms along with their recognition results comparison from the first Facial Expression Recognition Challenge.[4] For a comprehensive review of early facial expression recognition system before 1998, see Zhang et al. [1998].

Age Estimation

As the social culture evolves from one generation to another, the age of a user reveals considerable information about the user's communicative behaviors and cultural habits. Hence obtaining the age information of the user is very important for building adaptive and user friendly vision-based interaction. Humans adjust their communicative behaviors when interacting with people of different ages. As a soft biometric that is directly associated with the human face, the most promising means of estimating the age is through facial analysis.

Nevertheless, as pointed out in Fu et al. [2010], although there is a large body of research on aging synthesis, age estimation from facial images is a relatively less explored topic. The reason may be largely due to two factors. On the one hand, it is generally very difficult to collect a large aging database—it takes many years to collect the face photos of a person at different ages. On the other hand, the face aging process is a very personalized process, which brings many challenges when estimating age from face images.

Following the taxonomy of Fu et al. [2010], some previous works on human age estimation attempted to derive signatures from anthropometric models [Gunay and Nabiyev, 2007; Kwon and da Vitoria Lobo, 1994; Ramanathan and Chellappa, 2006]. The underlying idea is to derive geometric features from cranio-facial development theory on the development pattern of

---

[4]http://sspnet.eu/fera2011/

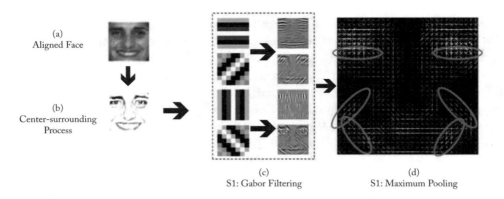

(a)
Aligned Face

(b)
Center-surrounding
Process

(c)
S1: Gabor Filtering

(d)
S1: Maximum Pooling

Figure 2.12: The extraction of the biologically inspired features proposed by Guo *et al.* [2009] (figure courtesy of Song *et al.* [2011]).

the human head over many years [Alley, 1988]. Specifically, Kwon and da Vitoria Lobo [1994] computed six ratios of distances on frontal faces and combined them with wrinkle patterns to differentiate adults from children. Ramanathan and Chellappa [2006] derived eight ratios of distance measures on frontal faces to model age progression on young faces from 0 to 18 years. Their goal was to leverage age estimation to help face recognition; a variant of these eight ratios had been adopted in [Gunay and Nabiyev, 2007] for age estimation. One intrinsic drawback of anthropometric model-based features is that they are only effective for young faces, as once they grow up, the geometric shape of adult faces will largely remain fixed.

Lanitis *et al.* [2002] approached this problem by defining an age function on top of an Active Appearance Model (AAM) [Cootes *et al.*, 2001]. Lanitis *et al.* [2004] subsequently evaluated and compared the performance of different classifiers for the task of age estimation on parameters estimated from the AAM model. Because the AAM model considers both shape and texture information rather than just geometric features, it is well equipped to handle faces across a range of ages.

Some more recent works have focused on identifying the age manifold. Geng *et al.* [2006, 2007] used a collection of sequences of personal face images over different ages [Geng *et al.*, 2006, 2007] with an extended principle component analysis algorithm that is able to deal with missing data entry. Fu and Huang [2008]; Guo *et al.* [2008]; Yan *et al.* [2009] employed mixed images from different persons at different ages. More specifically, Fu and Huang [2008] applied the conformal embedding method to build the age manifold, which proved to be effective in predicting ages from facial images. Guo *et al.* [2008] proposed a locally adjusted robust regression (LARR) method on an age subspace built from the orthogonal locality preserving projections (OLPP), and achieved a very high prediction accuracy of 5.07 years in mean absolute error (MAE) on the FG-NET database.[5] Yan *et al.* [2009] proposed a more complicated embedding method, namely synchronized submanifold embedding (SSE), for person-independent age estimation. It considers both the age labels and subject identities to improve the generalization. Nevertheless, it achieved inferior results (an MAE of 5.21 years) on the FG-NET database when compared with Guo *et al.* [2008]'s method.

Appearance- or feature-based methods seemed to have further pushed the benchmark performance in age estimation. For example, Yan *et al.* [2008] used a Gaussian mixture of spatially flexible patches to be the feature representation for age estimation, achieving an MAE of 4.95 years on the FG-NET aging database. Guo *et al.* [2009] used biologically inspired features (BIFs) derived from the HMAX model, a feedforward model of the primate visual recognition pathway. It achieved the best recognition accuracy on the FG-NET aging database reported so far: an MAE of 4.77 years using a Support Vector Machine on the BIFs. A more comprehensive recent effort is presented in Song *et al.* [2011], who leveraged the BIFs to train a universal multi-view age estimator through collaborative visual learning on face tracks from web videos and a small set of face images with labeled ages. The face track collection provided constraints that faces in the same track should have the same age. We refer the readers to Song *et al.* [2011] for details of their universal multi-view age estimation system, which is perhaps the best performing age estimator to date for vision-based interaction.

Due to its demonstrated performance, we present a few more details of the extraction process of the BIFs, as shown in Figure 2.12. The extraction of the BIFs is composed of three processing steps: the center-surround pre-processing, the S1 layer processing, and the C1 layer processing. The center-surround pre-processing step simulates the first step of human visual perception to highlight the local contrast, as illustrated in Figure 2.12 (b). The resulting contrast-enhanced face image is then processed by the S1 layer, which is convolved by a set of Gabor filters. The filter responses are then spatially pooled together using the max operator, which is the operation performed in the C1 layer.

2.2.2 EYES

Eye detection

Reliable eye detection [Belhumeur *et al.*, 2011; Haro *et al.*, 2000; Wang *et al.*, 2005] is a prerequisite for attentive vision-based interaction, serving as the first step to enable eye gaze/contact estimation. Accurately detecting and localizing an eye is often evaluated by how accurately the pupil center is estimated by the detection algorithm. Depending on whether or not special lighting sources are used, eye detection systems can generally be categorized into two approaches, active and passive detection.

Active detection methods often leverage near-infrared (IR) light to illuminate the eye [Haro *et al.*, 2000; Zhu *et al.*, 2002]. Under near-IR illumination, the eye pupil will present a unique bright/dark pupil effect due to its reflective spectral properties; this can be conveniently

[5]http://www.fgnet.rsunit.com/

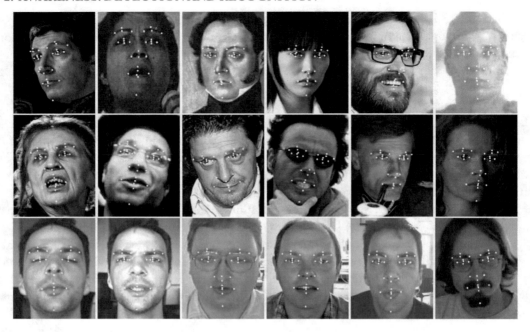

Figure 2.13: Sample face fiducial points estimation results using the method proposed by Jesorsky *et al.* [2001] (figure courtesy of Jesorsky *et al.* [2001]). First two rows presented the results in the LFPW dataset and the third row presented results on the BioID database. Note how accurate the eye positions are localized.

employed to detect the eye. These active detection methods can often produce accurate detection results in a controlled indoor environment. They may not be as feasible in outdoor settings, as the environmental natural light interferes with the IR light source.

Passive detection methods often take a pattern recognition approach, localizing the eyes from the unique visual patterns present in distinctive features in the image. Previous work has explored to identify unique eye patterns from image gradients [Kothari and Mitchell, 1996], various projection functions [Gan and Liu, 2010; Zhou and Geng, 2004], and shape templates [D'Orazio *et al.*, 2004]. These methods all take a bottom-up approach to detecting the visual pattern, either from heuristics or voting schemes such as the Hough transform. Some other works have built their eye detection systems by running more advanced statistical machine learning algorithms on low level image features to classify eyes and non-eyes. For example, Huang and Wechsler [1999] proposed to learn a Gaussian Radial Basis Function over selected optimal wavelet packets for classifying eye patterns. Feris *et al.* [2002] employed a two-layer Gabor wavelet network (GWN) learned from training data to localize fiducial facial features. Experiments on the FERET database showed that about 95% of eyes were located with a distance error less than 3 pixels. Some other works investigated the efficacy of Boosting a casacade classifier from Haar features [Ma et al., 2004] or more discriminative features learned from nonparametric discriminative analysis [Wang et al., 2005].

Most of these previous works regard eye detection as an isolated task, ignoring the inherent structure in human faces. In other words, there are strong structural constraints of different facial components, which may be reinforced if the detection of different facial components are performed jointly. Several previous works (e.g., [Belhumeur et al., 2011; Cao et al., 2012; Gu and Kanade, 2008; Liang et al., 2008]) have combined local component detection/matching and global structure regularization for accurate face fiducial points estimation and/or face alignment. In particular, Liang et al. [2008] incorporated a component-based discriminative search process into a global shape model, where the search direction is trained from labeled match/non-match image patches of each face component. Gu and Kanade [2008] posed a generative face shape prior in a hierarchical Bayesian framework for accurate face alignment. The global model used in these two methods for structure regularization are parametric models. Another work of note is the supervised descent method proposed by Xiong and la Torre [2013], which learns the descent direction on sampled data points in a supervised fashion to facilitate more efficient optimization of the nonlinear least square problem for detecting the various facial points.[6]

In view of limitations of parametric models, recently Belhumeur et al. [2011] presented a non-parametric exemplar-based approach for regularizing individual local part detectors. Its effectiveness has been demonstrated in a face image database collected from the Internet, namely Labeled Face Parts in the Wild (LFPW), and also further validated in the publicly accessible BioID database [Jesorsky et al., 2001]. It achieved state-of-the-art results on both datasets. Some example results are shown in Figure 2.13. Instead of taking an exemplar based approach, Cao et al. [2012] explicitly trained a regression function to estimate the shape of the face composed of the facial landmarks. It achieved even higher accuracy than the method proposed by Belhumeur et al. [2011]. Ideally, the tasks of face detection and other facial component detection (such as eye detection) should be jointly formulated in a unified task. Some recent work by Zhu and Ramanan [2012] has explored this idea, which showed some promising results.

Eye gaze estimation

Gaze estimation is intended to identify the point of a user's gaze in three-dimensional space or the visual axis of the eyes [Chen and Ji, 2011]. In human-computer interaction, eye gaze information has been utilized either as new and advanced computer input on its own [Jacob, 1991], or as complementary input to traditional input devices such as mouse pointers [Zhai et al., 1999].

Vision-based gaze estimation methods can generally be categorized into 2D mapping-based methods and 3D methods. The 2D mapping based methods [Morimoto et al., 2002; Tan et al., 2002; Zhu and Ji, 2004] attempt to learn a mapping from feature vectors, such as 2D pupil glint vectors induced from active near-IR lighting [Morimoto et al., 2002; Zhu and Ji, 2004] or

---

[6]Code available at http://www.humansensing.cs.cmu.edu/intraface

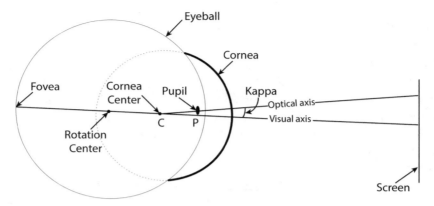

Figure 2.14: The structure of the eyeball (figure courtesy of Chen and Ji [2011]).

appearance of 2D eye images [Tan *et al.*, 2002] to the gaze direction or, in the typical case of eye gaze controlling a cursor, the gaze point on the screen. As summarized in Chen and Ji [2011], 2D mapping-based methods suffer from two drawbacks. Firstly, a careful calibration needs to be performed to tune the parameters of the mapping function. This may involve, for example, asking the user to look at several reference points on the screen. Secondly, even if calibration is performed, the head pose and position may still affect the accuracy of gaze estimation. This is because the 2D features may change significantly according to the head motion and position. Therefore, to ensure accurate gaze estimation after calibration, users will need to keep their heads still. This is not desirable as it poses unnatural constraints to the users.

In contrast, the 3D methods do not suffer from the issue of head pose and motion, as the visual axis is estimated from 3D features and the gaze point is obtained by estimating the intersection point between the visual axis and a scene object (e.g., a display screen). 3D gaze estimation methods either use a stereo camera [Beymer and Flickner, 2003; Chen *et al.*, 2008; Guestrin and Eizenman, 2008; Shih and Liu, 2004] or a single camera with a set of calibrated structured lights [Guestrin and Eizenman, 2006]. Although 3D gaze estimation methods can largely relieve the difficulties induced by head pose and motion, they still need a user-specific calibration process due to the mismatch of the optical axis and visual axis of human eyes, as illustrated in Figure 2.14.

As seen in the figure, the eyeball can be considered to be made up of two nested spheres of different sizes. The smaller anterior sphere segment is the cornea, which is transparent and hosts the pupil. The optical axis of the eye is defined as the 3D line connecting the center of the cornea and the center of pupil, while the visual axis is defined as the 3D line connecting the center of the cornea with the center of the fovea, which is the region of the fovea with the highest acuity. The gaze point is defined as the intersection of the visual axis with a scene object or point (e.g., a screen). Most 3D measuring can only directly recover the optical axis due to the anatomical structure of the eyes. To identify the visual axis, the angle between the visual axis and the optical axis, namely κ, needs to be modeled. However, the value κ is a person-dependent quantity. This is the fundamental reason why personal calibration is needed for 3D gaze estimation algorithms.

Traditionally, users need to look at some specific points on the screen to provide ground-truth gaze point to estimate κ for calibration. This is not a natural process. Recently, Chen and Ji [2011] proposed a probabilistic framework for more natural calibration of 3D gaze estimation. This is achieved by combining a 3D gaze estimation method with a visual saliency map, such as the one calculated by Harel et al. [2007]. In this framework, users do not need to look at a set of designated points; instead, they view a set of natural images. Through probabilistic modeling of the visual attention via the visual saliency map, the probability $p(\kappa)$ is estimated and factored into the 3D gaze estimation by Bayesian reasoning. This probabilistic framework achieved more robust estimation results comparing with traditional 3D gaze estimation systems largely due to the prior model of gaze through the visual saliency map and the probabilistic modeling of κ.

2.2.3 HANDS

Hand detection

Visual detection, segmentation, and tracking of hands are integral parts of a robust hand gesture recognition system. Previous work on visual hand detection largely falls into three categories: color-based methods, appearance- or shape-based methods, and spatial context-based methods. Color-based methods detect hands using skin color detection [Wu and Huang, 2000; Wu et al., 2000]. Many appearance- or shape-based approaches detect hands by Boosting a cascade detector with Haar features [Kolsch and Turk, 2004b; Ong and Bowden, 2004] similar to that of the Viola-Jones face detector [Viola and Jones, 2001]. These previous works have demonstrated success in controlled indoor environment and have been successfully integrated into vision-based interaction systems such as the HandVu system [Kölsch, 2004; Kolsch et al., 2004]. They have had limited success in dealing with visual data from unconstrained environments. Context-based methods [Buehler et al., 2008; Karlinsky et al., 2010; Kumar et al., 2009] exploit the spatial structural contexts of different parts and detect the positions of the hands by pictorial structure analysis, which has achieved some success in unconstrained settings.

In a more recent work, Mittal et al. [2011] presented a more comprehensive solution, which combines detection results from all three different types of detectors and forms a two-stage algorithm for hand detection. In the first stage, detection results from color, appearance or shape, and context are aggregated together to generate detection hypotheses. The hypotheses are then further scored by all three methods and a discriminative trained model is further leveraged to verify the hypothesis. By combining visual cues from different methods and the discriminative verification model, this system achieved very high precision on hand detection tasks even under unconstrained imaging conditions. To date, this approach achieves state-of-the-art results in hand detection.

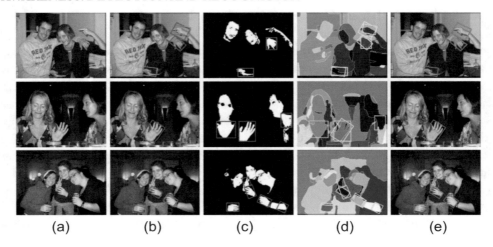

(a)   (b)   (c)   (d)   (e)

Figure 2.15: The overview of the hand detection method proposed in Mittal *et al.* [2011]: (a) The original image. (b) Some hypotheses produced by appearance- and context-based detector. Bounding boxes in red are proposed by the appearance-based detector and in green by the context detector. (c) Hypotheses generated by skin color-based detector. (d) Superpixel segmentation of the image hypothesized bounding boxes from the three detectors. By super-pixel-based non-maximum suppression (NMS), overlapping bounding boxes are suppressed. (e) Final detection results (figure courtesy of Mittal *et al.* [2011]).

Hand gesture recognition

Hand gesture recognition is one of the key components of a vision-based interface which provides a convenient means for non-intrusive human computer interaction. Robust hand gesture recognition is generally difficult to achieve due to visual sensors and lens variations, background clutter, lighting changes, and differences in users. To address these issues, a successful algorithm not only needs to build invariance in visual features to locate and represent the hand, but also requires a good classification model to recognize hand gestures from the features. Various visual cues have been explored in the past [Wachs *et al.*, 2011], including motion [Kang *et al.*, 2004; Shen *et al.*, 2011a,b], depth [Raskar *et al.*, 1998; Rauschert *et al.*, 2002], color [Hasanuzzaman *et al.*, 2004; Kolsch *et al.*, 2004; Rauschert *et al.*, 2002; Rogalla *et al.*, 2002; Yin and Zhu, 2006], shape [Belongie *et al.*, 2002; Cootes and C.J.Taylor, 1992; Freeman and Roth, 1995; Yin and Zhu, 2006], appearance-based methods [Hasanuzzaman *et al.*, 2004], and fusion of multiple cues [Kolsch *et al.*, 2004; Rauschert *et al.*, 2002].

As demonstrated by Kolsch *et al.* [2004]; Rauschert *et al.* [2002], fusing diverse visual cues can improve the robustness and accuracy of hand gesture recognition. Indeed, combining multiple visual cues together facilitates efficient separation of the hand from the background [Kang *et al.*, 2004], or focused feature extraction on the hand regions without explicit segmentation [Shen

Figure 2.16: The screenshot of the HandV visual gesture-based interface which integrates multiple visual cues for hand detection, tracking and recognition (figure courtesy of Wachs *et al.* [2011]]).

et al., 2011a,b], which subsequently provides cleaner data for recognizing the hand gesture. For example, the HandVu system developed by Kolsch *et al.* [2004] leveraged appearance and skin color for hand detection; the subsequent recognition of hand gesture is performed with both motion and color information. In terms of classification methods for gesture recognition, previous work has explored both rule-based methods and statistical machine learning-based methods including support vector machines (SVM), AdaBoosting, and more complicated temporal models such as Hidden Markov Models (HMM) and their variants. It is difficult to determine the best learning algorithm overall, but a general consensus is that modeling the dynamics of the hand gesture can help make more robust recognition. Hence temporal modeling techniques such as HMM may be better suited for this task. However, these techniques require more computation than static classifiers. When designing a hand gesture-based interface, most often we will need to make a trade-off between speed and accuracy due to real-time performance requirements.

Alon *et al.* [2009] presented a unified framework for both gesture recognition and spatiotemporal hand gesture segmentation. This unified framework presented a practical solution to real-world gesture recognition from RGB cameras, as most previous methods would assume that spatiotemporal segmentation has already been done. With the great success of the depth sensing Kinect camera, much recent work, such as Wang *et al.* [2012], has explored using the Kinect depth map for dynamic hand gesture recognition. Guyon *et al.* [2012] have built a benchmark dataset using a Kinect camera and conducted an initial evaluation of various gesture recognition algorithms, which represents the state-of-the-art results on gesture recognition from off-the-shelf depth sensing data.

Figure 2.17: Sample human detection results from the discriminative deformable part based model proposed by Felzenszwalb *et al.* [2010b]. The last two framed image results are false positive images (figure courtesy of Felzenszwalb *et al.* [2010b]).

We refer interested readers to Wu and Huang [1999] for a comprehensive review of gesture recognition research before 1999, and Mitra and Acharya [2007a] for a review of more recent work in hand gesture recognition.

2.2.4 FULL BODY

Body detection

Person detection from images and videos is among the most intensively studied topics in computer vision. Among all the visual complications which confront robust human detection, pose variation, local part deformation, and partial occlusion are among the most difficult. State-of-the-art scanning-window-based object detectors present the challenge of *feature misalignment* [Lin *et al.*, 2009], referring to the phenomenon that features detected in some positive detection windows may not be detected in the same location, or at all, in other positive detection windows.

Holistic methods [Dalal and Triggs, 2005; Maji *et al.*, 2008; Papageorgiou *et al.*, 1998b; Tuzel *et al.*, 2007; Zhu *et al.*, 2006] concatenate local visual descriptors in a fixed order, such as HOGs [Dalal and Triggs, 2005] or local binary patterns [Wang *et al.*, 2009], and then train a classifier to detect the human body pattern. Their performances are inevitably limited by feature misalignment. Part-based approaches such as Lin *et al.* [2007]; Mikolajczyk *et al.* [2004]; Wu and Nevatia [2005] attempt to address this issue by training part classifiers and integrating their responses. However, training a classifier for every part may be computationally expensive. Intuitively, adopting a part-based representation along with a holistic method, if appropriately modeled, may largely alleviate the feature misalignment issue.

Previous work [Dollar *et al.*, 2008; Felzenszwalb *et al.*, 2010a, 2008; Lin and Davis, 2008; Tran and Forsyth, 2007] has approached this problem by allowing object parts to scale and/or shift spatially for better feature alignment, and leveraging machine learning algorithms to determine the optimal configuration of the visual parts. However, most of these approaches manually choose the object parts to learn the configuration. There is no guarantee that the manual selection will be optimal for detection.

On the other hand, some boosting-based approaches [Laptev, 2006; Tuzel *et al.*, 2007; Wu and Nevatia, 2008; Zhu *et al.*, 2006] implicitly select visual parts, but they do not take feature misalignment into consideration. Meanwhile, multiple instance learning (MIL) [Pang *et al.*, 2008; Viola *et al.*, 2005] has been demonstrated to effectively handle object misalignment at the holistic level (i.e., the whole detection window). A natural question to ask is: can we extend the idea of multiple instance learning to handle the problem of feature misalignment? The answer is quite straightforward by allowing multiple instances at the part levels, which is the gist of the detection algorithms proposed by Dollar *et al.* [2008]; Lin *et al.* [2009]. These two algorithms can automatically learn discriminative parts for human detection. More importantly, the number of parts can be automatically determined in the training process under such a MIL-Boosting framework.

The discriminative deformable part-based model (DPM) proposed by Felzenszwalb *et al.* [2010a,b, 2008] is widely regarded as one of the best performing methods for human detection. It deals with feature misalignment by allowing the local part detector to operate on different locations instead of on a fixed location. Figure 2.17 presents some sample human detection results from this approach. The DPM model adopted a latent SVM learning framework. It determines the parts by a greedy heuristic strategy based on information obtained from the root filter, which is a holistic human detector operating on a coarse level of the image pyramid. One minor drawback of such a framework is that the number of parts must be pre-specified. How to automatically determine the number of parts under such a learning framework could be an interesting problem to explore.

Since state-of-the-art human detectors are all built upon modern machine learning techniques, there are some general observations from previous research on practices that should lead to better detection accuracy: (1) More training examples generally lead to more accurate detectors. Not only more positive examples, more difficult negative examples will also help train more accurate detectors. (2) A flexible representation, such as the DPM, can greatly facilitate dealing with the visual variation induced by pose variations. (3) More discriminative low-level image features, such as HoG [Dalal and Triggs, 2005], are important for more accurate detection.

Articulated body tracking and pose estimation

Robust estimation and tracking of full body pose is an essential step for full body gesture recognition. This has continued to be one of the most active research areas in computer vision, generating a significant literature (refer to Poppe [2007] for a survey of the literature before 2007).

Earlier work has largely focused on human sensing and pose estimation from images or videos produced by conventional video cameras. Various strategies have been exploited to tackle this challenging problem. For example, Bregler and Malik [1998] proposed to track human figures using twists and exponential maps. Ioffe and Forsyth [2001] presented two methods to generate plausible body segment configurations and to efficiently prune invalid configurations using projected classifiers. Body segment hypotheses are produced by grouping parallel edges. The pictorial structure method [Felzenszwalb and Huttenlocher, 2005] uses dynamic programming to effi-

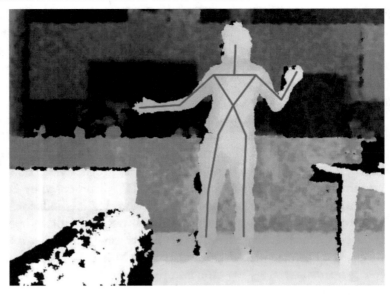

Figure 2.18: Skeleton tracking results with XBox Kinect (figure is obtained from http://learning. codasign.com/index.php?title=Skeleton_Tracking_with_the_Kinect).

ciently identify the best 2D configuration of human body parts. Mori and Malik [2002] took an exemplar-based approach by matching shape context descriptors. A parameter sensitive hashing method was proposed by Shakhnarovich *et al.* [2003] to facilitate fast nearest neighbor search for exemplar-based human pose estimation.

Wu *et al.* [2003] proposed using a dynamic Markov network to track articulated human motion, where inference is performed by using a mean field Monte Carlo algorithm. A similar part-based loose-limbed model was later on proposed by Sigal *et al.* [2004], where a non-parametric Belief Propagation algorithm was leveraged for resolving the inference problem in Bayesian tracking. Agarwal and Triggs [2004] presented a silhouette-based method for 3D body pose estimation; Hua *et al.* [2005] proposed a data-driven belief propagation approach to combine top-down and bottom-up reasoning together to estimate human pose. Ramanan *et al.* [2005] tracks human motion by initializing from a set of pre-defined key poses. Urtasun and Darrell [2008] proposed a local mixture of Gaussian processes to estimate human pose by regression. Bourdev and Malik [2009] proposed to use *poselets*, which are tight clusters in both 3D pose and 2D appearance, and trained from 2D images with 3D pose annotations to estimate pose by SVM classification.

Notwithstanding the demonstrated success of these works on human pose estimation and tracking from conventional camera sensors, the recent availability of inexpensive depth cameras has triggered a significant interest in research on robust human pose estimation from depth imagery [Anguelov *et al.*, 2005; Grest *et al.*, 2005; Knoop *et al.*, 2006; Plagemann *et al.*, 2010; Shotton *et al.*, 2011; Siddiqui and Medioni, 2010; Zhu and Fujimura, 2007]. In a system from Microsoft Research and Microsoft Xbox incubation [Shotton *et al.*, 2011], the XBox Kinect camera is exploited and a heavy data collecting and labeling effort is conducted to gather a large amount of depth image data with labeled poses. Largely due to the clean depth data, which significantly reduced the negative effects of the background clutter, Shotton *et al.* [2011] use a per-pixel classification scheme using randomized decision forest to assign each pixel to a specific body part.

Due to the high quality of the depth information, it was found that no further smoothing needs to be performed to achieve high accuracy in this per-pixel classification scheme. This pose estimation system has been used as part of the human body tracking system of the Xbox Kinect games, and millions of users have experienced hands-free control of video games, different from the LED tracking and accelerometer-based control used in the Nintendo WII. Figure 2.18 presented a screenshot of skeleton tracking results with Kinect cameras, to illustrate how the depth image looks and how the algorithm proposed by Shotton *et al.* [2011] works.

2.3 CONTEXTUAL HUMAN SENSING

We have presented systematic reviews of detection and recognition methods for various aspects of human sensing. These algorithms compose a solid technology foundation for building awareness sensing for vision-based interaction. We should emphasize, however, that human communicative behavior is context sensitive: the same body gesture may represent a completely different meaning in a different context. Contextual information could gathered and estimated from different sources, such as the users themselves, the task environment, and even the cultural norms. Effective visual sensing of people has to model all kinds of contextual information, some of which may not be able to be obtained through visual sensing alone.

Various components of visual human sensing may provide contextual information to one another. For example, the same hand gesture with different facial expressions may indicate very different user intentions or emotional status. Therefore, accurate awareness sensing in vision-based interaction must perform joint reasoning of the information from the various detection and recognition algorithms, which attempt to determine information about different aspects of the users. This integration process is necessary since all the detection and recognition algorithms we summarized in the previous section are context insensitive.

The environment, which includes the information about the location, the observed subject, and even the current task, also provides subtle contextual information. For example, the location of the interaction may largely determine the profession or goals of the user. The same gesture or facial expression may indicate different things when the performing users are of different professions. Hence, it is vital for a vision-based interface to be fed with sufficient information about the environment context. Without such knowledge, awareness sensing may be prone to failures caused by the lack of environmental awareness.

The cultural background of the users also provides vital information for vision-based interaction to accurately infer the user's behavioral state. For example, a head shake is a common gesture found in South Asian cultures such as India, which indicates "no problem" when performed. However, in a different culture, it may be interpreted in a completely different way.

In summary, to build robust awareness sensing to a vision-based interface, we have to take various contextual information into consideration. This facilitates not only more accurate recognition, but also more personalized and intelligent interface.

CHAPTER 3

Control: Visual Lexicon Design for Interaction

In the previous chapter, we discussed awareness sensing in vision-based interaction and the associated detection and recognition problems. In this chapter, we will focus our discussion on the *control processor* of a vision-based interface. Unlike awareness sensing, *control sensing* is intended to capture human communicative behaviors that are specifically intended for interaction with the system. In practice, the design of the control processor of a vision-based interface often starts with the lexicon—a set of (static or dynamic) visual patterns from various visual human sensing tasks. These visual patterns are subsequently mapped to specific commands for application control. The mapping may be done in two ways. The first maps each individual visual pattern in the lexicon to a control command. The second seeks to recognize a *sequence* of visual patterns in the lexicon to trigger a command, which is naturally a richer representation.

Although the lexicon design (or the selection of the visual patterns) varies from system to system, there are a set of general principles to be followed for lexicon design, in order to assure the usability of a vision-based interface [Wachs *et al.*, 2011]:

- **Learnability**: When designing a lexicon to control applications, one prerequisite condition is that the set of adopted visual patterns, such as gesture patterns, must be easy to perform and remember. This not only ensures that the users have a low overhead in learning and memorizing which gesture patterns map to which control commands, but also ensures that the visual patterns are conveniently performed and produced by the users when interacting with real applications.

- **Robustness and accuracy**: The adopted visual patterns for control purposes must be detected and recognized robustly and accurately. This is not only just about developing better vision algorithms, but also about designing visual patterns/gestures that are easily distinguished from one another, since similar visual patterns will be difficult to differentiate. How to design the lexicon in this way, with ease of detection and recognition in mind, is a very interesting topic of study.

- **Intuitiveness**: The visual patterns in the lexicon should have a clear cognitive association with the control functions to which they are mapped. For example, a closed circle formed by the thumb and the index finger with the other three fingers open may be interpreted as an "OK" sign. Of course, the meaning of a certain visual or gesture patterns may vary from culture to culture, so it may be appropriate to take the cultural background of the users into consideration when designing the lexicon. Other relevant factors may include the general knowledge and linguistic capability of the users.

- **Comfort**: Lexicon design should avoid visual patterns that can only be generated by exotic hand gestures or full body movements that require strenuous muscle tension over a long period of time. In other words, it must ensure the ergonomic comfort of the users. For example, if the system requires users to repeatedly raise their arms in horizontal positions, it may quickly cause fatigue or discomfort. This is commonly referred to as "Gorilla arm."

- **Reconfigurability**: A vision-based perceptual interface may be employed by users with a wide range of demographic backgrounds. It is therefore unrealistic to think that a single universal lexicon would work for all users. The lexicon design should be reconfigurable and be easily adapted and tailored to the preference of the users. This implies that for each control function we require a set of associated potential candidate visual or gestural patterns. In this way, users may personalize and reconfigure the lexicon by selecting from the candidate list.

Obviously, both static and dynamic visual patterns can be exploited for designing the lexicon for controlling applications. In the rest of this chapter, we review lexicon design in several state-of-the-art vision-based interfaces based on static and/or dynamic visual information. Our discussion will be largely focused on the lexicon design, but we will also cover how recognition is performed with a designed lexicon.

3.1   STATIC VISUAL INFORMATION

Static visual information often refers to the visual appearances produced by a static configuration of the body or body parts of the user, including static body/hand posture [Freeman and Weissman, 1995; Iannizzotto et al., 2005; Sachez-Nielsen et al., 2004; Stenger et al., 2010], posed facial expression [Abdat et al., 2011], attention and static eye gaze information [Jacob, 1991], etc. In the following, we review and discuss the lexicon designs and recognition algorithms that leverage each type of these static visual appearances.

3.1.1   LEXICON DESIGN FROM BODY/HAND POSTURE

As pointed out in Pavlovic et al. [1997], communicative gesture can be either acts or symbols. Acts are gestures that are directly associated with the interpretation of the movement itself. In contrast, symbols refers to those gestures that have a linguistic role, which can often be represented as a set of static hand postures. Because of this, gestural symbols are widely used in the context of human-computer interaction.

The River Rush game in the Xbox game *Kinect Adventures!* [Microsoft, 2010] provides a good example of lexicon design based on static body postures for vision-based interaction. Figure 3.1 presents a screenshot of the game. In River Rush, one or two players can control the

Figure 3.1: The Kinect River Rush game [Microsoft, 2010].

directions of the raft by leaning or moving left and right, and they can fly the raft by a simple jump. Therefore the lexicon in this game contains only three groups of visual patterns, namely *left*, *right*, and *up*. Specifically, to direct the raft to the left, players can either lean their bodies left or move a step leftward. Likewise, to direct the raft to the right, they can either lean to the right or move a step rightward. To fly the raft, players just need to make a simple jump. The recognition of these gesture patterns is achieved by detecting static postures on a per-frame basis. As discussed in the previous chapter, the body posture estimation in Kinect is achieved by per-pixel classification using a randomized decision forest [Shotton *et al.*, 2011]. The control lexicon in the River Rush game provides an example of a good design as the body postures adopted are easy to *learn*, *intuitive* to memorize, and *comfortable* to perform, just as what the users would perform in a real raft.

Many visual hand gesture based HCI systems have been proposed, such as Freeman and Weissman [1995]; Iannizzotto *et al.* [2005]; Sachez-Nielsen *et al.* [2004]; Stenger *et al.* [2010]. The system proposed by Freeman and Weissman [1995] is among the first of its kind, aiming to replace the infrared television remote controller with more natural vision-based gesture control. In this system, when a user wants to control the TV, he/she holds up his/her hand to face the screen. This is the "trigger gesture" designed in the lexicon. The system is constantly looking for the trigger gesture, even when the television is off. Once the trigger gesture is detected, the TV enters the control mode, which presents a hand icon on the screen to follow the user's hand movement. The hand is detected and tracked by template matching using normalized correlation on edge orientation histograms. To activate a control, the user needs to move the hand icon to be

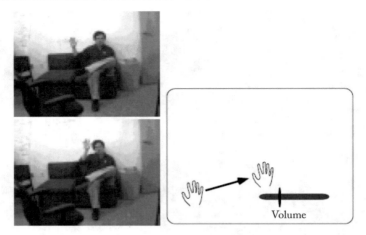

Figure 3.2: An illustration of the visual gesture based TV control system [Freeman and Weissman, 1995].

on top of the control and hover there for 200 msec. For example, if the user wants to adjust the volume, after the volume control is activated, the user can move his/her hand to slide the volume control bar to adjust it. When finished, he/she can either close his/her hand or simply move the hand out of the camera view to exit from control mode. Hence, the lexicon in this system only contains one main gesture pattern, i.e., the open and up hand, as shown in Figure 3.2. Although this prototype system was published more than 15 years ago, it was not until recently that major TV manufactures, such as Toshiba, Sumsung, and LG, began building visual gesture-based TV controls in their commercial products.

In Iannizzotto *et al.* [2005], a vision-based interface is designed to control a toy car. The system is equipped with two cameras. One camera captures the moving area of the toy car, where the captured video sequence will be projected to a transparent plexiglass panel coated with a special semi-transparent film for rear projection. The second camera tracks and recognizes the hand gesture operating on the panel to control the toy car. The setup of the system is presented in Figure 3.3(a).

Similar to the gesture-based TV control system by Freeman and Weissman [1995], this vision-based gesture control interface also leveraged a single gesture pattern to be the active control gesture. The specifically adopted hand gesture is the pointing finger gesture, as shown in Figure 3.3(b). All other gestures are considered to be neutral gestures. The fingertips are detected by a sequence of low-level image processing algorithms such as background subtraction, morphological filtering, contour analysis, etc. Hand gesture is recognized by firstly calculating the distances of the detected finger tips to the center of gravity of the hand silhouette, which are subsequently matched with statistics extracted from the training images. The hand is further tracked

(a) System set-up.

(b) The lexicon.

Figure 3.3: The physical system set up and the lexicon of the vision-based perceptual interface for controlling a toy car [Iannizzotto *et al.*, 2005].

by a Kalman filter, and the movement of the active hand gesture is exploited to control the toy car. Such lexicon design with a single active gesture makes the system easy to learn and use, and simplifies the recognition task to facilitate reliable real-time performance.

Of course, multiple gesture patterns may be desired or required in the lexicon. In the system proposed by Sachez-Nielsen *et al.* [2004], a visual memory subsystem (VMS) is introduced, which allows the users to define the set of hand gestures to be recognized for interaction. Each gesture in the lexicon will have multiple samples stored in the VMS. The recognition is performed by nearest neighbor search in terms of Hausdorff distance on edge maps. They conducted an evaluation of 26 gesture in the lexicon, achieving 90% average accuracy in recognizing these gestures.

Stenger *et al.* [2010] present a vision-based remote control system that enables users to have touch-free interactions with a display at a distance. To initiate the interaction, a user faces the camera on the display. The Viola-Jones face detector [Viola and Jones, 2001] is leveraged to detect the face. The user then can hold his/her hand in a fist pose near the face. The system uses an additional Cascade detector to detect the hand in fist pose. Once a fist is detected near the face of the user, the system uses a multiple cue visual tracker to robustly track the hand fist. To select, start, and interact with applications, their lexicon also includes the open hand pose and a thumb-up pose. To select an application icon and activate the application, the user can present an open hand or thumb-up pose and either hover over the icon for a short period of time or swing left and right with the fist pose. The open hand pose is also used to stop a video playing when the user is browsing a video collection. Figure 3.4 presents the lexicon used in Stenger *et al.* [2010]. Compared with systems with single gesture in the control lexicon, the lexicon used in Stenger *et al.* [2010] is more rich and hence can be reconfigured to tailor to the users' preferences. For

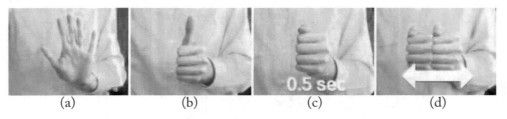

Figure 3.4: The lexicon adopted in Stenger *et al.* [2010].

example, some users may prefer thumb-up pose more than open hand and the system could be reconfigured by mapping the users' preferred pose to the intended control .

Many existing systems [Bretzner *et al.*, 2002; Freeman and Weissman, 1995; Ike *et al.*, 2007; Kolsch and Turk, 2004a; Robertson *et al.*, 2004], including the Xbox Kinect [Microsoft, 2010], use the hovering-over-for-a-period design to select and activate menu items or application icons. This appears to be a convenient choice as it does not require the system to recognize an additional hand pose. This reduces the number of visual gesture patterns that need to be recognized and subsequently helps to ensure the *robustness and accuracy* of the recognition algorithm. Many modern vision-based interfaces, including commercial systems such as the XBox Kinect, adopted a similar design to use hand-hover-for-a-period to activate and trigger a control on the screen.

3.1.2   LEXICON DESIGN FROM FACE/HEAD/FACIAL EXPRESSION

Although hand/body gesture-based human machine interfaces may be intuitive and preferrable, there are application scenarios which call for vision-based interaction without using hands. For example, a user's hand may be occupied by other tasks or otherwise unavailable, or a user may be temporarily or permanently disabled. In these scenarios, an alternative is to design vision-based interfaces based on visual input from a user's face, head, and even facial expressions. Examples include both academic research prototypes [Canada *et al.*, 2002; Fu and Huang, 2007; Kumar and Kumar, 2008; Toyama, 1998; Tu *et al.*, 2007] and industrial commercial products such as the CameraMouse[1] and Jamboxx.[2]

Fu and Huang [2007] presented a virtual mouse system called *hMouse* to control a cursor with head movement. They developed a detection driven head tracker that combines the Viola-Jones face detector [Viola and Jones, 2001] and a skin color-based tracker [Bradski, 1998]. The yaw, tilt, and roll rotation of the head is estimated from the tracking results. The system handles four different categories of virtual mouse events including *hold and release, move cursor, fine position to point*, and *left/right button click*. The lexicon defined to trigger these mouse events involves different head movements. In particular, the forward and backward movement of the head with

---

[1]http://www.cameramouse.com/
[2]http://www.jamboxx.com/

respect to the camera is used to trigger the *hold* or *release* event. If the tracked head size exceeds 80 pixels in the 640×480 video frame, it triggers the mouse hold event; otherwise, the mouse release event is triggered. The cursor move event is triggered by the 2D position changes of the tracked head rectangle in the video frame. The *fine positioning* of the cursor to a specific point on the screen is adjusted by the tilt and yaw angle of the head, relative to the neutral position. Finally, the left/right button click events are triggered when the roll angle is less than -0.6 radian (left button click) or larger than 0.6 radian (right button click). The lexicon design is subject to several manually specified parameters such as the size of the head in terms of pixels. This renders the learnability of the control lexicon not to be that great.

Tu *et al.* [2007] proposed a camera mouse, a vision-based interface using 3D face tracking, where 12 facial action units from the facial action coding system (FACS) [Ekman and Friesen [1978]] is adopted as the control lexicon. Unlike the *hMouse* system, the camera mouse can operate in three different modes: *direct mode*, *joystick mode*, and *differential mode*. In the first two, the cursor position is directly mapped based on the head pose to the screen, which is somewhat correlated to the user's focus of attention. The differential mode tracks the relative motion of the face and incrementally updates the position of the mouse cursor on the screen. The 3D facial tracking allows more flexible design of the lexicon to trigger button-click events with mouth motions detected in the non-rigid facial motion parameters. For example, the detection of mouth opening will trigger the left-button-click event, while the detection of mouth corner stretching will trigger the right-button-click event. Figure 3.5 shows the system setup and a screen-shot while playing Solitaire. The rich control lexicon designated from the 12 facial action units makes the system highly *reconfigurable*. In contrast to the Ad-Hoc lexicon design of the *hMouse* system, the lexicon design of the camera mouse system is well motivated from and grounded by the anatomical structure of the facial muscles. One potential issue is that accurately tracking the 12 facial action units from videos is a non-trivial task, which inevitably affects the robustness and accuracy of the system.

Facial expression conveys important information about a user's emotional state, which is important in some vision-based interaction contexts. However direct use of facial expression for application control is a relatively less explored area. Abdat *et al.* [2011] presented a system that exploits facial expression recognition to control a music player. The authors built an anthropometric model and combined it with the Shi and Tomasi [1994] algorithm to track and localize facial feature points in the detected face rectangle. For facial action coding [Ekman and Friesen, 1978], the authors represented each facial muscle by a pair of key points. The state of each muscle is subsequently encoded by the change in the distance between the key points in the current expression, compared with the corresponding distance in the reference neutral face. The facial expression hence comprises the states of all the facial muscles.

An SVM classifier is trained to recognize six facial expressions: happy, fear, anger, sadness, surprise, and neutral. For controlling the music player, the control lexicon includes all six facial expressions. In their system, whenever facial expressions associated with negative affect are de-

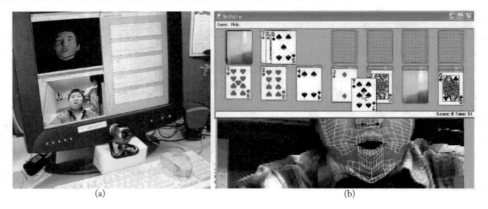

Figure 3.5: The camera mouse system [Tu *et al.*, 2007]: (a) the system setup; (b) the screen-shot of using the camera mouse system to play Solitaire (courtesy of Tu *et al.* [2007]).

tected, the music player changes the music being played in an effort to steer the user's affect into a positive state. We anticipate that vision-based interfaces based on facial expression recognition may play an important role in helping severely disabled individuals, for whom even moving the head become a difficult task. One potential issue with facial expression-based lexicon design is that it may not be that *comfortable* for the users to switch from different contrived facial expressions. Nevertheless, the *learnability* of such a vision-based interface is very high as users would already know how to make certain facial expressions.

3.1.3   LEXICON DESIGN FROM EYE GAZE

There is a long history of research which attempts to exploit eye gaze information for intelligent human-computer interaction [Goldberg and Kotval, 1999; Hutchinson *et al.*, 1989; Jacob, 1993, 1991; Kim and Ramakrishna, 1999], detecting and tracking eye gaze in real time. As we discussed in the previous chapter, eye gaze is directly associated with a user's focus of attention. Hence it can be used to provide context for other vision-based sensing. For example, Chau and Betke [2005] combined eye tracking with eye blink detection, where the blink action is used as a single action lexicon to trigger the mouse click event at the location provided by the gaze location.

If no other facial or eye patterns are leveraged, one commonly adopted method to enable interaction with eye gaze is to measure how long the user has stared at an object on the screen. For example, if the user looks at an icon on the screen beyond a minimum period of time, then the icon can be activated. Early work by Jacob [1993, 1991] has compared using eye gaze to select an object on the screen with using the mouse to select it. Their study shows that using eye gaze is not only more convenient, but also faster. In this eye gaze-based system, tracking the eye gaze is similar to moving the mouse cursor using the hand. The action of looking at an object on the screen for a period of time is the same as clicking the button on the mouse; hence the lexicon for control is composed of a single action.

Eye gaze-based interaction has been helpful for severely disabled users, such as quadriplegics who are unable to move their heads freely, providing them a means to gain some independence and control. The stare-over-a-period lexicon design in a way is similar to the hand-hover-a-period design. Hence such a system should be very *easy to learn* and *intuitive to use*. One potential caveat of an eye gaze-based interface is that humans are sensitive to the surrounding environment, so if the environment is highly dynamic, the users' attention and hence eye gaze may easily get distracted. This may affect the *robustness and accuracy* of the system and suggests that an eye gaze lexicon-based control interface may better be used in a static environment.

3.2   DYNAMIC VISUAL INFORMATION

One limitation of using static information for vision-based interaction is the need to form a posed gesture for a period of time in the interaction process. This may be somewhat contrary to a user's natural communicative behavior. Many previous works have also explored the use of dynamic visual gestures for interaction. Mitra and Acharya [2007b] provides a comprehensive overview of recent gesture recognition methods, which discussed both static and dynamic gesture recognition.

As summarized in Shen *et al.* [2011c, 2012], the approaches to dynamic gesture recognition can be categorized into two types: model-based and exemplar-based. For model-based approaches, Hidden Markov Models (HMMs) are perhaps the most frequently used models [El-gammal *et al.*, 2003; Marcel *et al.*, 2000; Rajko *et al.*, 2007; Wang *et al.*, 2006b; Yamato *et al.*, 1992]. In Yamato *et al.* [1992], dynamic feature vectors are transformed to symbolic sequences by vector quantization, then subsequently modeled by a discrete HMM. Marcel *et al.* [2000] trained an Input-Output HMM using Expectation Maximization (EM) and applied it to recognize gestures from the hand silhouette extracted by segmentation and tracking. Some recent improvements over traditional HMMs include the semantic network model (SNM) [Rajko *et al.*, 2007], the non-parametric HMM [Elgammal *et al.*, 2003], and the Hidden Conditional Random Field [Wang *et al.*, 2006b]. These models either reduce the training efforts or improve the classification accuracy.

Other model-based approaches include Finite State Machines (FSM) [Davis and Shah, 1994; Hong *et al.*, 2000], dynamic Bayesian Networks (DBN) [Suk *et al.*, 2008], and topology-preserving self-organizing networks [Flórez *et al.*, 2002]. All of these approaches assume that the hand has been detected and its articulated motion is tracked, either achieved by skin color segmentation or kinematic model-based hand tracking [Bretzner *et al.*, 2002]. Although they present promising results, the robustness of the approaches is largely limited by the difficulties of hand motion tracking and detection. Additionally, it is both data intensive and computationally prohibitive to train these models before they can be applied for recognition.

To circumvent the difficulties of hand tracking and detection, other approaches try to leverage invariant visual representations and matching of example gestures for recognition. For

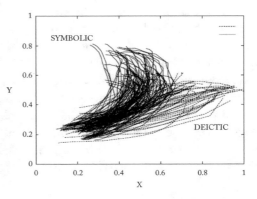

(a) Hand and face blobs

(b) Deictic and symbolic gesture paths.

Figure 3.6: Lexicon design in a body-face space: (a) the face and hand blobs tracked, and (b) the deictic and symbolic gesture paths in the body-face space (courtesy of Marcel *et al.* [2000]).

example, Yang *et al.* [2002] directly extract motion trajectories for matching example gestures; Kirishima *et al.* [2005] extract Gaussian Density Features in regions surrounding selected interest points for learning and matching; Freeman and Roth [1995] proposed that spatio-temporal gradients of image intensity may be useful for dynamic gesture recognition. More recently, Chaudhry *et al.* [2009] calculated a sequence of histograms of oriented optical flow and used Binet-Cauchy kernels on nonlinear dynamical systems to achieve state-of-the-art in periodic human action recognition. In general, the larger the exemplar database, the better the recognition accuracy is likely to be.

In the rest of this section, we focus our discussion on control lexicon design with dynamic gestures, presenting some representative works in both model-based and exemplar-based approaches.

3.2.1   MODEL-BASED APPROACHES

Either explicitly or implicitly, model-based approaches for dynamic gesture recognition quantize the dynamic feature vectors into symbolic sequences by vector quantization. A dynamic gesture pattern composed of symbolic sequences is then modeled by a generative or discriminative dynamic probabilistic model such as an HMM (and its variants) [Elgammal *et al.*, 2003; Marcel *et al.*, 2000; Rajko *et al.*, 2007; Yamato *et al.*, 1992] or a Hidden Conditional Random Field Wang *et al.* [2006b]. Here we summarize how some of these approaches design their control lexicon, and we refer the reader to the corresponding papers for more details of the specific proposd algorithms.

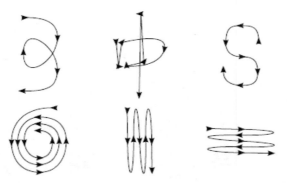

Figure 3.7: The six gesture recognized in Rajko *et al.* [2007] using the semantic network models (courtesy of Rajko *et al.* [2007]).

Marcel *et al.* [2000] proposed to use an Input-Output Hidden Markov Model to recognize two types of gesture paths in the body-face space, i.e., deictic and symbolic gestures. As they state, "the deictic gestures are pointing movements toward the left (right) of the body-face space and symbolic gestures are intended to execute commands (grasp, click, rotate) on the left (right) of the shoulders." The hand and face regions are tracked as skin color blobs; based on the location of these two blobs, a user-specific body-face space is built based on a discrete space for hand location centered on the face of the user. This user-body space is built using an anthropometric body model expressed as a function of the total height of the user, calculated from the height of the face. The gesture path is defined as the 2D trajectory of the hand-blob during a gesture. Figure 3.6 presents an illustration on how the body-face space is formed by tracking the skin blobs of the hand and face (Figure 3.6(a)), and how the deictic and symbolic gesture paths are defined over the body-face spaces. It may take some efforts for the user to learn how to exactly perform the two types of gestures as it involves both the hand and the face. On the other hand, the deictic and symbolic gesture paths both are associated with a group of dynamic movements—this provides a lot of flexibility for the users to perform the gesture in their own way and hence have the potential to provide personalized experiences to them.

Rajko *et al.* [2007] proposed an extension of HMM, namely the Semantic Network Model (SNM), for visual gesture recognition. The SNM introduces the so-called semantic states to indicate, for example, the start and end of a gesture, which do not produce any observations. It reduces the complexity of general HMMs in the sense that it exploits the common factors in the state transition probabilities and hence reduces the number of parameters that need to be estimated. Figure 3.7 presents the six different pen gestures recognized in this work, which naturally composes a visual gestural lexicon for control purpose. The pen gestures in this lexicon are designed

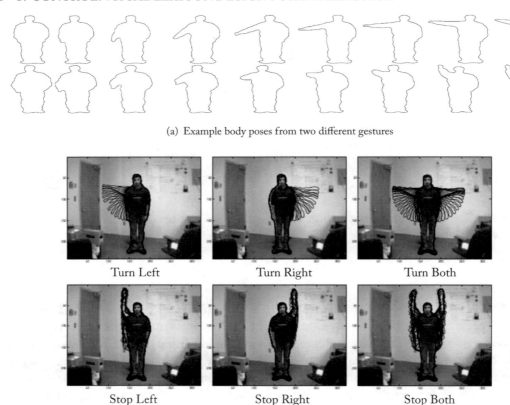

(a) Example body poses from two different gestures

Turn Left   Turn Right   Turn Both

Stop Left   Stop Right   Stop Both

(b) SixFullBodyGesture.

Figure 3.8: Example body poses (a) and a six gesture lexicon (b) used in Elgammal *et al.* [2003] (courtesy of Elgammal *et al.* [2003]).

in such a way that they are naturally discriminative to one another. However, they may be too complicated for any users to learn—i.e., the learnability of the lexicon is low.

Elgammal *et al.* [2003] proposes to use an HMM to learn the dynamics over a large exemplar space using a nonparametric estimation approach for exemplar-based recognition. Each gesture is then represented as a sequence of learned body poses (exemplars). Strictly speaking, this method can also be categorized as an exemplar-based approach, since the learned nonparametric HMM is used to represent the dynamic information in each gesture. We nevertheless discuss it here due to the technical formulation it adopts. The shape of the human body silhouette is leveraged as the visual representation. Figure 3.8 presents some example body poses in the database used to learn the nonparametric dynamics (Figure 3.8(a)) and a six-gesture lexicon (Figure 3.8(b))

Figure 3.9: The six gestures tested in Wang *et al.* [2006b]. From left to right, the six gesture categories are: FB - Flip Back, SV - Shrink Vertically, EV - Expand Vertically, DB - Double Back, PB - Point and Back, EH - Expand Horizontally (courtesy of Wang *et al.* [2006b]).

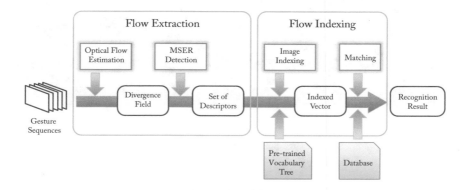

Figure 3.10: The processing pipeline of efficient motion pattern matching with divergence image (courtesy of Shen *et al.* [2012]).

adopted in Elgammal *et al.* [2003]. These six full-body gestures are intuitive to perform although some of them require relatively large space.

HMMs and their variants are generative models, which model the joint distribution of the observations and the dynamic gesture labels. When applied to classification problems to recognize dynamic gestures, discriminative models, where the probability of the gesture label given the visual observations is directly modeled, may be more desirable due to the issue of limited training examples. Wang *et al.* [2006b] extend the conditional random fields (CRF) model proposed by Lafferty *et al.* [2001], namely the Hidden Conditional Random Fields (HCRF), to incorporate a hidden layer between the visual observation and the gesture label to better bridge the semantic gap. Wang *et al.* [2006b] conducted experiments on a gesture database composed of a lexicon of 6 gesture classes, as shown in Figure 3.9. The HCRF model compares favorably to HMMs and

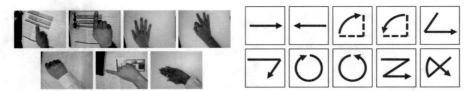

(a) Seven postures: thumb, index finger, hand, hold, fist, index finger with 90° rotation and hand with 90° rotation.

(b) Ten dynamic gestures: move right, move left, rotate up, rotate down, move down-right, move right-down, clockwise circle, counter-clockwise circle, "Z", and cross.

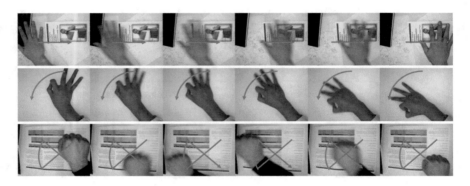

(c) Some examples in the database.

Figure 3.11: The 10 dynamic gestures (posture independent) composes the control lexicon. An exemplar database with 10 categories of gestures and 1,050 samples in total is collected (courtesy of Shen *et al.* [2012].

the basic CRFs. These six gestures involve relatively more complicated movement of both hands, hence it may take more effort for the users to learn them. However, the increased complexity of the hand movement makes the gestural patterns more discriminative to each other. Hence it helps maintain the robustness and accuracy of the system.

3.2.2   EXEMPLAR-BASED APPROACHES

To improve real-time performance, some research efforts have focused on speeding up image and video processing by either designing more efficient algorithms [Lockton and Fitzgibbon, 2002] or leveraging a more powerful computing unit [Chen *et al.*, 2003a] such as the GPU. Some other approaches [Shen *et al.*, 2011c, 2012] have focused more on building scalable visual representations of dynamic gestures, which enables scalable matching of a query to a large database of exemplars.

Shen *et al.* [2011c, 2012] proposed a new visual representation of dynamic hand gestures based on the divergence field of the flow motions, which transforms gestural motion patterns into spatial image patterns. Given a gesture sequence, the flow motion field between any two consecutive frames is extracted. Its divergence field is further obtained. Salient spatial patterns such as Maximally Stable Extremal Regions (MSER) [Forssen and Lowe, 2007; Matas *et al.*, 2002] from the divergence fields are detected. A descriptor is subsequently extracted from each detected region to characterize the local motion patterns. The descriptors extracted from all example gesture sequences are indexed by a pre-trained hierarchical vocabulary tree. A new gesture sequence is recognized by matching against the database with a TF-IDF scheme [Nistér and Stewénius, 2006], which is scalable to large scale databases. The pipeline of this method based on divergence map is illustrated in Fig. 3.10.

This method is a first attempt to transform motion patterns into spatial image patterns using divergence field. The spatial patterns are then encoded by local motion descriptors. This enables leveraging state-of-the-art image indexing techniques for scalable hand gesture recognition without resorting to hand detection, segmentation, or tracking. A database of dynamic hand gestures with 10 categories and 1,050 samples was constructed for evaluation. The lexicon of 10 dynamic gestures is shown in Figure 3.11(b). The recognition rate of the motion divergence method on this evaluation dataset is 97.62%, with an average recognition time of 34.53ms. This method presents not only a novel approach to motion pattern analysis, but also a scalable framework for dynamic hand gesture recognition with a large number of examples. One of the advantages of the 10 dynamic gestures adopted in the control lexicon of Shen *et al.* [2011c, 2012] is that they are independent of the posture of the hand. So the users can comfortably perform it in any hand posture and even holding an object in the hand. This makes the system highly reconfigurable to be tailored to the users' personal preferences.

Note that the exemplars do not need to be extracted from real visual examples. They could be, for example, a set of pre-defined motion templates. Such simple motion templates have been explored by the PEYE system [Hua *et al.*, 2007] and the TinyMotion system Wang and Canny [2006] for vision-based interaction on mobile devices. Two such motion patterns defined in the PEYE system are presented in Figure 3.12. The algorithm proposed in PEYE tracks the motion of four pixel blocks in each video frame, and the combination of these four motion vectors defines a unique motion gestural pattern. It is shown that such visual motion-based mobile interaction presents great benefits for a wide variety of mobile applications including web browsing and mobile gaming. We point out that the lexicon designed in the PEYE system not only incorporated visual motion gesture patterns, but also leveraged other visual patterns such as dark view, de-focus blurring, etc. We refer the readers to Hua *et al.* [2007] for more details. This control lexicon composed of a set of motion template is easy to learn and intuitive to be conducted on the mobile phone, which makes the mobile vision gestural-based interfaces of high usability.

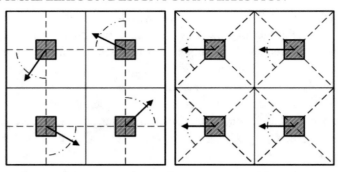

Figure 3.12: Two motion gesture patterns "rotate clockwise" and "move right" defined in the PEYE system (courtesy of Hua *et al.* [2007]). The PEYE system tracks the motion vectors at four locations and the combination of these four motion vectors defines the corresponding motion pattern. The arcs indicate the direction ranges the motion vectors should fall into.

3.3   COMBINING STATIC AND DYNAMIC VISUAL INFORMATION

As we have discussed, a vision-based interface should ideally embrace both static and dynamic visual information in order to provide rich and broadly useful interaction. For example, the lexicon of American Sign Language (ASL) is composed of a set of static postures and dynamic hand motion trajectories of the two hands. More than 6,000 gestures, as well as finger spelling, are exploited to represent common words, communicating obscure words, and proper nouns. Even some non-manual features, such as movements of the faces and the torso, also play a very important role in ASL. One would imagine that a subset of ASL could effectively serve as the lexicon for vision-based interaction. An important issue is then how to effectively recognize ASL components based on visual input.

Much previous work has attempted to tackle this important problem, including [Starner *et al.*, 1998] and [Vogler and Metaxas, 2001, 1998, 1999]. Advocated by Starner *et al.* [1998], the Hidden Markov model [Rabiner, 1979] (HMM) has become the most popular modeling tool for ASL recognition, as it largely relieves the sequence segmentation problem. (For those interested in a detailed introduction to HMMs, see the seminal paper of Rabiner [1979] for theories and algorithms of HMMs.[3]) Although we confine our discussion to ASL recognition, the algorithms and technologies we discussed here are generally applicable to recognizing other sign languages, such as various European sign languages [Efthimiou *et al.*, 2009], Chinese sign language [Gao *et al.*, 2004], etc.

---

[3]For some online resources include a Matlab library, the reader may refer to http://www.cs.ubc.ca/~murphyk/Software/HMM/hmm.html

(a) SWP ASL recognition system with views from desk mounted camera.

(b) SWP ASL recognition system with views from hat mounted camera.

Figure 3.13: The two SWP ASL recognition systems with: (a) a desk mounted camera, and (b) a hat mounted camera (courtesy of Starner *et al.* [1998]).

In this section, we will focus on introducing some of the early seminal works using HMMs for recognizing American Sign Language. In particular, we will discuss the SWP [Starner *et al.*, 1998] and the VM [Vogler and Metaxas, 1998] systems for ASL recognition. Both systems attempted to recognize a subset of words of the full ASL lexicon. These already enabled them to have a much more rich lexicon than any of the systems we have discussed already using either static or dynamic information, but not both. As one can imagine, the learnability of a rich lexicon naturally decreases but the reconfigurability would naturally increase. So there is balance to strike between these two. Meanwhile, the increased size of the lexicon may lead to less robust and less accurate recognition, due to increased subtlety among the various visual gestures. One way of resolving this issue is to hierarchically group these visual gestures to form a multi-level lexicon. That way, we do not need to recognize two visual gestures that are otherwise too difficult to differentiate by working at the appropriate level of the lexicon.

3.3.1 THE SWP SYSTEMS

The SWP ASL recognition systems described in Starner *et al.* [1998] are two real-time HMM-based systems for recognizing sentence-level continuous ASL of a 40-word lexicon. The first system observes the user from a desk-mounted camera, i.e., the camera is observing the user from a third-person viewpoint. The second system exploits a hat-mounted camera looking downward. To some extent, it appears that the camera is observing the user from the first-person point of view. The 40-word lexicon recognized in both systems include 6 pronouns, 9 verbs, 20 nouns, and 5 adjectives. A four-state HMM is trained with approximately 400 sentences and subsequently tested on 94 sentences. In both systems, the hand blob is obtained by skin color detection and segmentation. The hand blobs are tracked and a 16-dimensional feature is extracted to represent each hand blob by second moment analysis. This 16-dimensional feature includes each hand's x

Figure 3.14: A visual example of 3D tracking of the arm of the user from a multi-view camera setting (courtesy of Vogler and Metaxas [2001]).

and y position, change in x and y positions between frames, area (in pixels), angle of axis of least inertia found by principal component analysis on the blobs, the length of the leading eigenvector, and the eccentricity of the bounding ellipse [Starner *et al.*, 1998]. Both the left and right hand blobs are assigned a 16 dimensional vector. When there is only one blob detected, which indicates that there is cross occlusion between the two hands, the same feature vector is assigned to both hands.

Both systems achieved above 90% accuracy in testing. The first person view setting achieved higher recognition accuracy compared to the third-person view setting. One potential reason is that the video taken from the hat-mounted camera is less susceptible to occlusions since the camera is observing the two hands from top-down. The great interest in the soon-to-be-released Google Glass[4] suggests that such a wearable platform may be ideal for sign language-based visual perceptual interface.

3.3.2   THE VM SYSTEM

Vogler and Metaxas [1998] presented an ASL recognition system that leveraged a model-based 3D tracking system to recover the rotation and translation of each segment of the user's arm. Figure 3.14 presents a visual example of the 3D tracking results from a three-view camera setting. The VM ASL recognition system takes the input from the 3D visual tracking and casts it in a set of context-dependent HMMs, leveraging the Bakis topology [Rabiner, 1979] as shown in Figure 3.15. In the Bakis topology, each state is connected to itself, the next state, and the state after the next. Previous work in using HMMs for time sequence modeling both in speech recognition and sign language recognition suggest that the Bakis topology can better cope with signing speed and phoneme lengths. We refer the readers to the details of the model in [Vogler and Metaxas, 2001, 1998] for more details of the HMMs used in the VM ASL recognition system.

The VM ASL recognition system can recognize a 53-word lexicon, which includes 8 pronouns, 15 verbs, 21 nouns, and 5 adjectives, and 5 other signs. The training and testing are con-

---

[4]http://www.google.com/glass/

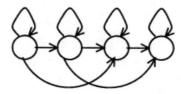

Figure 3.15: The example of a 4-state HMM with the Bakis topology (courtesy of Vogler and Metaxas [2001]).

ducted on a corpus of 486 continuous ASL sentences. Each of the sentences is between 2 and 12 signs long, with a total number of 2,345 signs. The system achieved above 85% recognition accuracy. Due to some limitations of HMMs, such as the inability to weight different features and degenerate performance with insufficient training, the VM system also combined pure visual template matching-based recognition with HMM-based recognition and demonstrated that such a combination can enhance the performance. To tackle the scalability issue of applying HMMs to large vocabulary ASL recognition, Vogler and Metaxas [2001] proposed to break down the signs into phonemes and model them with *parallel HMMs*.

3.4   DISCUSSIONS AND REMARKS

Recent decades have shown substantial progress in computer vision research in support of vision-based interaction for application control, culminating in recent commercial devices such as the Microsoft Kinect and the Leap Motion Controller, which support accurate full body motion tracking and hand motion tracking, respectively. Clearly not all successful systems are based solely on traditional RGB camera sensors. Instead, many are both modifying the sensor and leveraging active lighting in the invisible (near-infrared) spectrum to enable robust matching with structured patterns. This has led to robust correspondences across a variety of scene variations, albeit with certain limitation (such as primarily indoor and close-up use). We emphasize that such high robustness and accuracy is required by VBI applications, making these devices well-suited to the domain.

From another perspective, although vision-based interaction presents many advantages and benefits, it only represents one modality of sensing. For some problems and environmental conditions, vision-based sensing may not be the best solution. Therefore, a comprehensive *perceptual interaction* approach, embracing the integration of multimodal sensory information, may provide the best user experience. By integrating multiple sensing modalities, systems can provide more robust sensing and interfaces that adapt to the environment—e.g., allowing some modalities to take over where others may fail. For any sensor-based interaction or control, it is important to give users constant and useful feedback so that they can have a sense of the progress of the interaction. We will have a more extensive discussion on multimodal integration in the next chapter.

CHAPTER 4

Multimodal Integration

We interact with the physical world multimodally, with both parallel and sequential use of multiple perceptual modalities such as vision, hearing, touch, balance, and proprioception to passively and actively explore our environment, to confirm expectations about the world, and to perceive and communicate new information. Multiple sensing modalities provide a wealth of information to support interaction with the world and with one another.

In contrast to our experience with the natural world, human-computer interaction has historically been focused on unimodal communication, focused on a single mode or channel, such as text on a screen using a keyboard for user input. Multimodal interaction seeks to create technologies, interaction methods, and interfaces that leverage natural human capabilities to communicate via speech, gesture, touch, facial expression, and other modalities, bringing more sophisticated pattern recognition and classification methods to systems for interaction. This is fundamentally an interdisciplinary endeavor, requiring collaboration among computer scientists, engineers, social scientists, linguists, and many others who seek to provide deep understanding of the user, the system, and the interaction context in order to provide compelling, useful multimodal interaction.

Multimodal interfaces aim to deliver natural and efficient interaction capabilities that may be preferred by users over unimodal alternatives, offer better flexibility and reliability, and offer interaction alternatives to better meet the needs of diverse users. Other advantages and potential benefits of multimodal interfaces are addressed by Oviatt and colleagues [Oviatt *et al.*, 2000, 2005]. Multimodal systems vary along several primary dimensions or characteristics, including [Turk and Kölsch, 2004]:

- The number and type of input modalities;

- The number and type of communication channels;

- Ability to use modes in parallel, serially, or both;

- The size and type of recognition vocabularies;

- The methods of sensor and channel integration;

- The kinds of applications supported.

As mentioned in Chapter 1, Bolt's 1980 "Put-That-There" demonstration [Bolt, 1980] provided useful insight into the value of integrating sensing modalities. The "put" act indicates a command describing a certain action to be taken to effect change in the physical world. While

Figure 4.1: Bolt's "Put That There" system [Bolt, 1980].

gesture may be useful to signal action when there is a very limited vocabulary of possibilities, language is much better suited to communicate a desired action or command when there are many options. "That" and "there" refer to an object and a location, respectively—spatial information that can be difficult to easily and accurately communicate verbally. In this example, neither the verbal utterance nor the visual gesture is adequate to communicate the necessary information alone—rather, both are needed to succinctly convey the user's intent. The binding of "that" to a particular displayed object and of "there" to a particular location on the screen provides an example of multimodal integration, merging or fusing the information provided by multiple modalities into a coherent, meaningful communication.

Since some modalities are better suited to efficiently communicating certain types of information, the selection of modalities for a particular context and the strategies employed for integration are important aspects of any multimodal system. Some modalities provide information at sparse, discrete points in time (e.g., a pointing gesture) while others generate continuous but less time-specific output (e.g., facial affect). Some modal combinations are intended to be interpreted in parallel, which others may typically be offered sequentially.

A critical question in multimodal integration involves the level at which integration should take place. Given streams of data from different modalities (e.g., voice, vision-based gesture, touch), should the data be processed separately and interpreted unimodally before being integrated with information from other modalities? This is a *late integration* model, or *decision-level integration*, merging the multimodal information only after unimodal processing and classification have taken place. Alternatively, perhaps the sensed data should be integrated across modalities immediately—an *early integration* model, or *feature-level integration* of sensory data. In between lies the option of *mid-level integration*, which allows for some amount of processing and classification before merging across modalities. There are advantages and disadvantages of these various levels in terms of training requirements, sequential (rather than simultaneous) use of modalities, and the level of semantic independence of the channels. There may be much to learn from studies of how biological sensory information is integrated (e.g., Coen [2001]) and an understanding of cross-modal influences in perception (e.g., Shams and Kim [2010]).

For surveys on various aspects of multimodal interaction, see Jaimes and Sebe [Jaimes and Sebe, 2007], who survey multimodal HCI research, with a particular emphasis on computer vision; Dumas *et al.* [2009], who cover multimodal principles, models, and frameworks; and Lalanne *et al.* [2009] who review fusion engines for multimodal input.

4.1   JOINT AUDIO-VISUAL ANALYSIS

Vision-based interaction technologies have been used in multimodal interaction in several ways, but the most common has been to combine a visual modality with speech. Face-to-face human interaction is fundamentally bimodal in nature, with audio and visual channels both playing important roles in how people communicate in person. A significant portion of the research in multimodal interaction has focused on the modalities of speech and vision, using vision-based interaction technologies to detect, recognize, and track the speaker and to perceive gestures, facial expression, and other body movements in the context of spoken conversation. Facial expression (including facial gesture) is often used in conversation to modify or contextualize what is being said—e.g., to indicate uncertainty or to exaggerate the affective content of the utterance—or to provide a clear, non-verbal signal to accompany or replace verbal communication. Semiotic gestures communicate meaningful information to the interactive dialogue—as opposed to ergotic gestures, which manipulate the environment, and epistemic gestures, which are used to discover the environment through tactile experience. McNeill [1992] defined four semiotic gesture types:

- Iconic: Representational gestures depicting some feature of the object, action, or event being described—e.g., object size, shape, or direction of motion.

- Metaphoric: Gestures that represent a common metaphor, rather than the object or event directly—e.g., scratching one's head to indicate confusion.

- Beat: Small, formless gestures, often associated with word emphasis.

- Deictic: Pointing gestures that refer to people, objects, or events in space or time.

These are all seen commonly in human-human interaction, and a system that can recognize these and integrate the non-verbal channel with the speech channel may be more natural and better able to understand a wide range of user intent. Aspects of the visual channel that are of particular relevance to meaning include spatial, pathic, symbolic, and affective information [Hummels and Stappers, 1998].

Some of the earliest work in audio-visual analysis for human-computer interaction was in the area of audio-visual speech processing (AVSP) [Potamianos *et al.*, 2004; Vatikiotis-Bateson and Kuratate, 2012], or speechreading, which acknowledges the important role vision can have in understanding speech. Sumby and Pollack [1954] first demonstrated over half a century ago that viewing a speaker's face can facilitate improved perception of acoustically degraded speech. This is commonly experienced in what is known as the *cocktail party effect*, where people intuitively focus more of their visual attention on a speaker's face and lips in a noisy environment in order to better understand what is being said. As opposed to full lipreading, the goal of speechreading is to provide an additional and somewhat independent sensing channel to help reduce uncertainty, to help disambiguate the speech recognition process. A well-known demonstration of the power of speechreading in the interpretation of speech is the McGurk effect [McGurk and MacDonald, 1976], in which adding a semantically conflicting visual signal to audio can alter the hearer's perception of a phoneme. This is generally viewed as evidence for interdependence of auditory and visual modalities in people.

Petajan [1984] developed one of the first audio-visual speech recognition systems in 1984, and there has been much research in this area over the years, including approaches that utilize simple 2D lip motion features, detailed 2D and 3D lip models, and full face appearance models to integrate with speech processing via hidden Markov models, Bayesian networks, and other statistical approaches. As with most multimodal integration research, the key questions are what visual features and parameters to compute, at what level to integrate the modalities, and how to generalize to new users without onerous (or perhaps any) user-specific training sessions. For a recent summary of work in the area, see Bailly *et al.* [2012]. In addition to integrating audio and visual channels for speech recognition, there has been significant recent interest in analysis and understanding of human emotion using visual and auditory cues [e.g., Nicolle *et al.* [2012]].

4.2   VISION AND TOUCH/HAPTICS

Vision-based interaction alone may be awkward or unnatural for users if they are required to make movements in space without the benefit of real-world physical constraints, without the feedback normally provided by physical contact and proprioception. Integrating haptic (touch- or force-based) feedback with VBI provides an opportunity to make the physical interactions more realistic and intuitive—for example, experiencing contact with solid objects, or at least a physical sensation that roughly approximates the appropriate contact, when hitting a ball or reaching the edge of a virtual display surface.

Figure 4.2: The AIREAL device for tactile experiences in free air [Sodhi *et al.*, 2013a].

Several mobile devices such as phones, tables, and game controllers, use subtle vibrations of the device timed to precisely coincide with touching the device's screen or reaching certain locations on the screen; a similar idea can be applied in 3D free-form movement if the haptic (vibration) devices can be work by the user and its vibration can be coordinated appropriately with hand or finger locations tacked by VBI technologies. Ye *et al.* [2003] integrated vision and haptics modalities in the context of augmented reality, using a PHANToM force feedback device from SensAble Technologies (now Geomagic) to simulate haptic interaction.

AIREAL, a recent prototype by Sodhi *et al.* [2013a] is intended to complement vision-based interaction by providing tactile sensations in mid-air without requiring the user to wear a physical device. The device (see Figure 4.2) enables users to feel virtual objects and experience textures in free space using vortices of compressed air pressure to stimulate the user's skin.

4.3 MULTI-SENSOR FUSION

In addition to integrating VBI technologies with other perceptual modalities, it can be useful to employ additional sensors that are not particularly aligned with human sensing abilities, in order to deliver robust vision-based interaction capabilities. For example, thermal infrared (IR) sensing is quite effective for detecting humans based on the emission of photons due to body temperature, rather than reflected light. Thermal IR has also been used for face recognition (for reviews, see Kong *et al.* [2005] and Martin1 *et al.* [2011]), both using IR alone [Buddharaju *et al.*, 2007], and integrating it with visible imagery [Bebis *et al.*, 2006; Chen *et al.*, 2003b]. Facial expression analysis may also integrate visible imagery with thermal IR [Wang and He, 2013; Wang *et al.*, 2010]. Near-infrared (which senses reflected IR energy, not emissive thermal energy) has also been used recently for facial expression recognition [Zhao *et al.*, 2011].

Non-imaging inertial sensors such as the accelerometers and gyroscopes that are typically found in mobile phones have been used in motion analysis [Thiemjarus *et al.*, 2012] and gesture recognition [Mace *et al.*, 2013] and for interaction scenarios such as gaming [Yang *et al.*, 2011] and health monitoring and rehabilitation [Amini *et al.*, 2011], Weenk *et al.* [2013] applications. There is also an increasing amount of research that integrates these sensors with computer vision methods for estimating pose, gesture, and activity. These sensors provide information on acceleration and orientation that can be employed either as independent sources to be integrated with vision-based estimation of movement or pose [Huang and Fu, 2008], or to provide constraints to limit the solution space of the vision-based methods [Paucher and Turk, 2010]. There is a longer history of integrating visual and inertial sensors in the robotics community (e.g., Dias *et al.* [2007]).

Eye-tracking systems can be coupled with body motion tracking to provide world coordinate frame estimates of gaze (e.g., Essig *et al.* [2012]), integrating two visual modalities that serve to complement one another. A well-known problem with interfaces based on eye-tracking is the so-called *Midas touch* problem, describing the difficulty of determining user intent based purely on gaze; a more general VBI system can help to disambiguate intent based on gestures or other body movement, thereby reducing or eliminating the problem.

CHAPTER 5

Applications of Vision-Based Interaction

Vision-based interaction technologies have many applications, in areas as diverse as security and surveillance, gaming and entertainment, consumer imaging, marketing, and many more. The ability to interact with people based on visual information includes image-based methods to detect people, locate and track them, identify them, determine their static or dynamic body positions, classify their facial expressions, estimate their visual focus of attention, recognize their gestures, read their lips, estimate personal characteristics (such as age, sex, and race or nationality), and classify their overall activity. A VBI system delivers its output to an interactive application that uses the static and/or dynamic information about the user to update its user model, providing awareness of the user and/or control information relevant to the application. The VBI system should be able to receive feedback from the application, helping to direct its focus and modify its performance. Figure 1.1 in Chapter 1 presented a summary of this interaction model.

In this chapter we present a brief overview of the state-of-the-art of vision-based interaction in several application scenarios and a discussion of some of the key new and promising commercial VBI systems.

5.1 APPLICATION SCENARIOS FOR VBI

Video Games   Modern electronic or video gaming provides a highly interactive environment in which players interact with devices and receive real-time feedback via video, audio, and haptics. Gaming PCs and consoles include high-performance sound cards and graphics cards whose development have been driven by the huge gaming market, estimated to be $24.75B in the United States in 2011[1] and $65B worldwide.[2] A game controller—which may be a keyboard, mouse, joystick, or dedicated gaming device with multiple input methods—is used to provide user input, typically to control game characters and objects.

The opportunities for vision-based interaction with video games are manifold, from detecting and recognizing user for automatic login to personalization of avatar appearance to gesture-based control of user movement and actions. Ideally, the visual sensing and perception should be transparent to the user, requiring no special actions by the user or constraints on movement or on game strategy. A VBI component may map its output to the syntax of the controller, replacing its

---

[1]The Entertainment Software Association, http://www.theesa.com/facts/
[2]"Factbox: A look at the $65 billion video games industry," Reuters article, June 6, 2011.

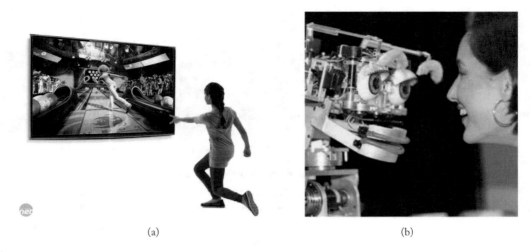

(a)   (b)

Figure 5.1: Two applications of vision-based interaction: (a) An Xbox Kinect bowling game. (b) Human-robot interaction.

functionality or providing an alternative input method, or it may offer a new model of interaction with finer-grained control of player movement and game action.

Since PC or console-based video gaming is typically done in a living room-like setting (indoors, with a limited area of movement), VBI solutions take advantage of these constraints; most do not work in more general outdoor environments with a wider range of illumination and movement possibilities. As gaming outgrows this environmental constraint, moving beyond the living room and becoming more mobile, vision-based interaction that support unconstrained movement and hands-free interaction may be even more desirable, but the challenge of extending VBI capabilities in less constrained environments is significant.

Mobile Interaction and Augmented Reality   With the advent of smartphones and tablets, mobile computing has become the main driving force in computing, supplanting the desktop as the primary computing environment in terms of mindshare, application development, web access, and number of devices. However, with the benefits of mobility and continuous access come the challenges of how to effectively interact with mobile devices without the traditional full-sized, physical keyboard, mouse, and monitor. Alternative input methods exist for mobile devices, such as one-handed chording keyboards (e.g., the Twiddler,[3]) and of course multi-touch capabilities provide useful selection and a limited range of gestural inputs. There has been a significant emphasis on speech interaction for mobile devices (e.g., with Apple's Siri and Google Now) to bypass the much slower physical or virtual keyboard interaction. New wearable devices such as Google

---

[3]www.handykey.com

Glass may help to spur greater interest in vision-based interaction in both live and offline search contexts.

Given these input limitations, there are opportunities to enhance mobile interaction using vision-based interaction methods, often in concert with speech and/or touch, primarily focusing on the user's face (via a device's front-facing camera) and on the user's hands (via the rear-facing camera). A wearable device such as the highly anticipated Google Glass may allow for two-handed gestural input, while a held device such as a smartphone is better suited to one-handed input. Early examples of real-time hand-based interaction for mobile augmented reality include HandVu [Kolsch et al., 2004] and HandyAR [Lee and Hollerer, 2007].

A form of augmented reality of great interest to retailers, and especially apropos to vision-based interaction, is the virtual fitting room, providing an interactive "magic mirror" try-on experience to a consumer at home or at the store. The ability to track and model faces (for virtual makeup or glasses) and bodies (for clothing) has the potential to reduce costs, to make the shopping experience efficient and effective, and to reach new customers.

Accessible Interfaces and Rehabilitation   Computer vision can be an alternative input modality for people with limited ability to use traditional interface mechanisms, whether due to physical impairments (e.g., due to medical conditions or age) or to environmental constraints (e.g., scenarios where looking at a screen or interface device is not possible or advisable). VBI technologies to determine eye gaze direction, hand movement, gestures, torso movement, etc., seek to translate feasible user movements into useful command and control information. Eye and gaze tracking, for example, has been used for several years to provide pointing and selection capabilities to disabled users who cannot operate a mouse, keyboard, or joystick.

Vision-based interaction has already begun to play a very important role in the rehabilitation therapy of stroke survivors. For example, the mixed reality stroke rehabilitation systems developed at Arizona State University [Chen et al., 2011; Lehrer et al., 2011a,b] use a set of cameras to capture the hand/arm movements of a stroke patient in either clinical or home settings. The visually captured motion is compared with a normal motion profile to quantitatively evaluate the progression of the rehabilitation through therapy. Depending on progress of the patient, the mixed reality multimedia system can provide continuous feedback to either encourage or discourage certain movements performed by the stroke patients. As in similar settings (e.g., in education), any media feedback to discourage behavior needs to be carefully designed and delivered in order not to frustrate the participants. More generally, vision-based interaction technologies can improve healthcare in several ways—e.g., as automated assistants to monitor patients in hospitals, people in assisted living situations at home, etc.

Human-Robot Interaction   Robots are increasingly viewed as devices that should interact with people, rather than as machines that replace people altogether. Factory floor robots used in manufacturing, autonomous and semi-autonomous vehicles, robot soldiers, robots in health and medicine environments, and personal robots (toys and companions) all need to interact with the people around them. Human-robot interaction seeks to leverage VBI technologies to allow robots to behave in safe and socially acceptable ways—to avoid people or to seek them out, to identify their owner or an intruder, to recognize signals and commands at a distance, and to recognize and react appropriately to their human companion's expressions. For overviews of this area, see Goodrich and Schultz [2007] and Kanda and Ishiguro [2012].

Smart Home/Office/Classroom and Instruction   Smart environments seek to adapt to human needs and behaviors in order to provide efficient and effective service, to minimize resource consumption (such as energy for lighting), to monitor adherence to a task or success in an activity, to maximize the comfort level and minimize stress of the people in the environment, etc. Such environments may use VBI technologies to keep track of the locations and identities of multiple people, to determine focus of attention, or to provide feedback on physical performance, from mouth and lip position for foreign language instruction to the mechanics of one's golf swing.

Human Behavior Analysis   Automatic analysis of human behavior has long been of interest to sociologists and others studying human interaction and communication. For example, analyzing human conversation and the use of gesture, facial expression, eye gaze, posture, and other non-verbal signals is important in order to understand the semantics of face-to-face communication—including such aspects as turn-taking—in general human-human interaction, including important areas such as child development and parent-child interaction. This has traditionally required painstaking, labor-intensive manual annotation of recorded video sessions. Automating this process has the potential to advance this kind of research significantly, allowing for much larger datasets and more precise, higher-dimensional annotated data, and providing more opportunity to study interaction *in situ*. Other areas of application include autism and psychiatric research, human factors and ergonomics research, usability testing, and consumer behavior research. Analyzing driver behavior, especially to determine focus of attention, fatigue, and drowsiness, is of great interest to the automobile industry to increase road safety.

There are several good surveys of research in human behavior analysis, including Pantic *et al.* [2007] and Borges *et al.* [2013].

5.2   COMMERCIAL SYSTEMS

No matter the application, vision-based interaction requires cameras or camera-based devices that can effectively sense the environment in the expected range of imaging conditions and provide robust, real-time output that can be used to enhance the intended application. Not long ago, this required building a system from scratch—choosing a camera, a method for getting digital image/video data swiftly into a computer, and a dedicated machine for running the vision-based algorithms. In recent years, however, there has been a significant change in the availability of relatively inexpensive sensors and systems to provide vision-based interaction capabilities, primarily driven by gaming and largely motivated by the success of the Nintendo Wii, introduced in late 2006, which included the Wii Remote ("Wiimote") motion controller. While not falling within

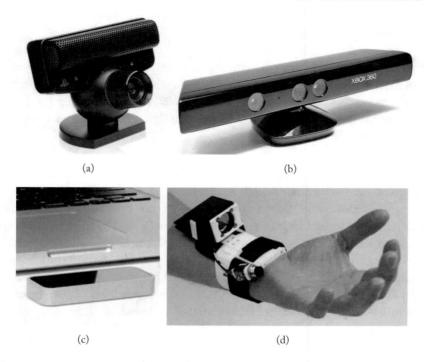

Figure 5.2: Some recent commercial devices for vision-based interaction: (a) Sony PS3 Eye Camera. (b) Microsoft Kinect. (c) Leap Motion Controller (next to a laptop). (d) Microsoft Digits.

our definition of a vision-based interaction device, the Wiimote provided gesture recognition and pointing input in a hand-held (one-handed) device equipped with a three-axis accelerometer in concert with a sensor bar connected to the game console. To determine the pointing direction, an image sensor on the Wiimote detects near-infrared LEDs on the static sensor bar, resulting in accurate pointing at distances up to about five meters. The Wiimote created great interest in sensing user movement in the context of interactive gaming.

Some key VBI devices that have recently become available or are likely to soon be available include:

Sony EyeToy and Eye Camera   The EyeToy, introduced by Sony in 2003 for the PlayStation 2, is a webcam that allowed PS2 players to interact with games using color-based background/foreground segmentation and user motion. Sony and other gaming manufacturers created many games specifically to leverage the visual and gestural interaction capabilities of the EyeToy, including sports, exercise, adventure, and combat games. The EyeToy requires a well-lit room for robust performance; several games use the EyeToy to include a live view of the player in the game or to map the player's face onto a game character, an example of what is often referred to as *augmented virtuality*.

Sony's successor to the EyeToy, the PlayStation Eye Camera, was introduced in late 2007 for the PS3 platform. The Eye provides better resolution and framerate than the original EyeToy, with a higher quality sensor array and more VBI capabilities, including face recognition, head tracking, and limited facial expression analysis. In 2009, Sony introduced the PlayStation Move motion controller, a hand-held, Wiimote-like device that can be tracked by the Eye to provide addition game control functionality.

Kinect The Microsoft Kinect for Xbox 360 debuted in late 2010, with a second generation device introduced for the new Xbox One in 2013. The first generation Kinect includes an RGB camera and a 3D depth sensor, based on technology from PrimeSense, which uses a projected pattern of infrared energy and an infrared sensor, providing full RGBD information (along with a microphone array and a pan/tilt unit). From the video frame rate of 640x480 in RGB and depth, with an 11-bit depth resolution, the Kinect software provides face detection and recognition, body modeling, and gesture recognition. Its range limit is approximately one to three meters, and it is generally limited to indoor environments due to the higher level of near-infrared energy (and thus interference with the IR sensing) from the sun in outdoor settings.

The second generation Kinect uses a different technology for depth sensing: a time-of-flight camera that promises higher spatial resolution (1080p) and accuracy. At its introduction in May 2013, Microsoft demonstrated much improved body modeling and gesture recognition, as well as heart rate tracking based on precise face tracking and changes in facial color Wu *et al.* [2012].

The Kinect supports a wide range of commercial games—in areas such as sports, dance, fitness, and adventure—that use body position and gestures to control characters, explore environments, and support the assessment of user activity. It has been used extensively as a general-purpose 3D sensor to support interactivity (e.g., Baricevic *et al.* [2012]; Sodhi *et al.* [2013b]), and its kinematic body tracking capability has been used for a wide range of interactive applications such as art installations.[4]

Leap Motion Controller The Leap Motion Controller, released in 2013, is a small device that tracks a user's hands and fingers (or held objects such as a pencil or a pointer) in a small area, reportedly with very high accuracy, using a pair of cameras and three infrared LEDs. Although just becoming available on the market as of this writing, the Leap device has generated a huge amount of interest in the VBI, human-computer interaction, and gaming communities, and it may serve to complement both touchscreen interaction and Kinect-like full-body interaction with very fast and low-latency dexterous, intuitive hand-based control, extending far beyond gaming applications into general human-computer interaction.

---

[4]See, for example, http://www.creativeapplications.net/tag/kinect/

Digits   The Digits invented at Microsoft Research Cambridge[5] is a wrist-mounted motion sensor intended to capture the full 3D gesture of the hand, as shown in Figure 5.2(d). The sensor is largely inspired by the success of Kinect. It does not require a line of sight with a receiver to work, and it can easily be programmed to recognize a wide range of hand gestures. It is acknowledged that the Digits device adopted similar depth sensing technology as Kinect, and hence is able to capture the full pose of the hand action the user is carrying out in real time. It is expected that the Digits device could replace a mouse, enable 3D spatial interaction with a mobile device, and complement existing input methods such as typing on a keyboard or swiping on a touch screen.

Systems for Human Behavior Analysis   Commercial eye tracking technologies have been available for many years, but recent years have seen significant improvement in accuracy, allowable range of motion, mobility, and cost. These systems typically use the corneal reflection of an infrared source, along with the location of the pupil center, to help determine the eye orientation. Lightweight, wearable eye trackers allow for mobility, but may be less accurate than fixed-position trackers. A limited form of gaze detection—whether or not the user is looking at the device—is beginning to show up in popular smartphones, such as the Samsung Galaxy S4, introduced in 2013.

There are several small companies that offer, or plan to soon offer, systems to analyze human behavior (including facial expressions and affect) for a range of application areas, such as Noldus, Affectiva, 3DiVi, and Machine Perception Technologies.

SDKs and open-source initiatives   In addition to sensing devices, there has been recent effort in building tools and environments (e.g., SDKs and libraries) to support the development of vision-based interaction capabilities and applications. The OpenNI consortium was formed in 2010 to promote and standardize natural interaction (NI) devices, applications, and middleware. Open Perception is a nonprofit organization aiming to support the development of open-source software for 3D perception. Intel has been pushing perceptual technologies for delivering natural, intuitive, and immersive user experiences via its Perceptual Computing SDK. Microsoft provides a Kinect for Windows SDK; PrimeSense offers NiTE, a middleware library for natural interaction.

---

[5]http://www.engadget.com/2012/10/09/microsoft-research-digits-3d-hand-gesture-tracking/

CHAPTER 6

Summary and Future Directions

Vision-based interaction is a broadly defined area that includes challenging problems in real-time image-based detection, tracking, modeling, and recognition in dynamic interactive environments, often in concert with additional sensing modalities. Unlike many other computer vision problems and domains, the focus on people—rather than on inanimate, and often rigid, objects—makes the problems more difficult and, for some, more interesting to work on. As we have discussed, there are many areas of application for VBI technologies that are being pursued, and undoubtedly many more that will be introduced by creative application developers as the component technologies continue to mature.

The past 20 years or so has seen tremendous interest and progress in the core VBI areas of face detection and recognition, facial expression analysis, eye tracking and gaze estimation, body tracking and modeling, gesture recognition, and activity analysis, primarily due to three factors: exponential growth in computing capacity, driven by Moore's Law advances in hardware; continuous advances in general computer vision algorithms and experimental methods, including the prominent role of machine learning and statistical methods throughout the field; and advances in the specific VBI component algorithms and methods motivated largely by the potential for real-world applications. Some specific methods and devices—e.g., Eigenfaces [Turk and Pentland, 1991a], Viola-Jones face detection [Viola and Jones, 2001], the Microsoft Kinect [Shotton et al., 2011]—have helped to generate interest and provide opportunities for students, researchers, and developers to experiment with VBI technologies over the years.

Despite the impressive progress in this area, there is still much work to do before vision-based interaction can reach the level of robustness and generality that is required to meet the promise of providing natural interaction in a wide range of environments and conditions. Most of the video-based methods are quite sensitive to lighting conditions and may fail when the conditions vary from what is expected. Depth-based methods tend to have limited range from the sensor and in some cases do not work outdoors. Humans can vary in appearance tremendously, due to changes in clothing, hairstyles, makeup, facial hair, glasses, age, etc.; modeling and compensating for these short- and long-term changes is still a very challenging set of problems. Some VBI methods depend on particular views (e.g., a frontal face view for face processing). Self-occlusion can be problematic.

Perhaps more fundamentally, some of the VBI technologies, such as gesture recognition, facial expression analysis, and activity analysis, have a complex relationship with the semantics of affect, intent, and application context. This is seen in the confusing terminology of "expression" vs. "emotion" as mentioned in Chapter 1.1. While there has been collaboration with researchers in communication, sociology, linguistics, and other related areas that study human behavior (e.g., Bartlett *et al.* [2000]; Quek *et al.* [2002]; Scherer *et al.* [2012]; Striegnitz *et al.* [2005]), so far these interactions have been limited in number and have had relatively little impact on real systems due to the complexity of the problems. These sorts of broadly interdisciplinary interactions that bring a deeper understanding of human behavior and context are important for long-term progress in the field.

Progress in computer vision, and especially in vision-based interaction, has benefited greatly by the availability of shared data sets to allow for apples-to-apples comparisons of methods. However, good and thorough data sets with accurate ground truth can be quite difficult and time-consuming to create, and there is always the danger of developing *to the data set* and thus missing key aspects of the more general problem. Limited data sets over-constrain the problem and lead to systems that only address a subset (and perhaps the easiest subset) of the problem. This has been seen in face recognition (with most work still focused only on frontal views), facial expression analysis (with a limited set of often posed expressions), and in gesture recognition and activity analysis (with a small set of pre-segmented and uniform-length gestures or actions). The field would benefit greatly from a thorough discussion of, and commitment to developing, public data sets, with an emphasis not just on *more* or *larger* data sets, but on data sets that are a good fit with the actual contexts in which VBI systems are to be used.

The availability of affordable depth sensors has made a tremendous difference in this area, and sensor systems for specific VBI tasks (such as eye tracking and hand/finger tracking) have a plethora of uses if they are both robust and non-obtrusive. The recent employment of eye gaze detection in mobile phones, such as Samsung's "Smart Scroll" and "Smart Pause" functionality, is a nice example of a widely deployed, consumer-friendly special-purpose VBI technology. Whenever a specific function becomes reliable and commonplace, developers find creative uses for them, often beyond the expectations of those inventing the technologies.

Meanwhile, the popularity of lightweight and fashionable wearable devices such as Google Glass[1] and smart watches from Sony[2] and Samsung may bring about a natural bridge between the physical world of the user and the cyberworld. This new generation of smart devices provides new opportunities for VBI technologies and, at the same time, poses additional challenges that are often neglected from a design perspective, such as how to ensure that the gesture lexicon adopted for control is socially acceptable or socially graceful.

Unlike in traditional HCI or VBI applications, where most often the user is interacting with the system alone and in an office or living room, the focus of a wearable VBI system needs to be more user-centered and context appropriate, with human factors as a primary consideration. One may want to avoid using gestures with dramatic motions, as interpretation from the social-

---

[1] http://www.google.com/glass
[2] http://www.sonymobile.com/us/products/accessories/smartwatch/

behaviorial point of view may not be that pleasant. Hence, in the design process, we should look into more subtle gesture lexicons.

While research in computer vision has constantly pushed the frontiers of "looking at people" from conventional imaging sensors and has enabled more and more VBI applications, we anticipate that future advances in VBI will be drastically transformed by: (1) new imaging sensors that capture more visual information beyond RGB pixels; (2) new mobile and wearable computing devices that go beyond conventional smart mobile phones and desktop computers; (3) new design principles beyond functional design that focus more on the users themselves; and (4) new techniques from other domains beyond computer vision to enable more robust fusion of multimodal information. The new design principles and new techniques from other domains will require cross-disciplinary research between computer vision researchers and researchers from other domains including interface design.

Bibliography

Abdat, F., Maaoui, C., and Pruski, A. (2011). Human-computer interaction using emotion recognition from facial expression. In *Computer Modeling and Simulation (EMS), 2011 Fifth UKSim European Symposium on*, pages 196 –201. DOI: 10.1109/EMS.2011.20. 48, 53

Agarwal, A. and Triggs, B. (2004). 3d human pose from silhouettes by relevance vector regression. In *Computer Vision and Pattern Recognition, 2004. CVPR 2004. Proceedings of the 2004 IEEE Computer Society Conference on*, volume 2, pages II–882–888. DOI: 10.1109/CVPR.2004.1315258. 44

Ahonen, T., Hadid, A., and Pietikainen, M. (2004). Face recognition with local binary patterns. In *Proc. of 8th European Conf. on Computer Vision*, Prague, Czech Republic. DOI: 10.1007/978-3-540-24670-1_36. 16

Alley, T. R., editor (1988). *Social and Applied Aspects of Perceiving Faces*. Lawrence Erlbaum Associates, Hillsdale, NJ. 34

Alon, J., Athitsos, V., Yuan, Q., and Sclaroff, S. (2009). A unified framework for gesture recognition and spatiotemporal gesture segmentation. *Pattern Analysis and Machine Intelligence, IEEE Transactions on*, 31(9), 1685–1699. DOI: 10.1109/TPAMI.2008.203. 41

Amini, N., Sarrafzadeh, M., Vahdatpour, A., and Xu, W. (2011). Accelerometer-based on-body sensor localization for health and medical monitoring applications. *Pervasive and Mobile Computing*, 7(6), 746–760. DOI: 10.1016/j.pmcj.2011.09.002. 72

Anderson, K. and McOwan, P. W. (2006). A real-time automated system for the recognition of human facial expressions. *IEEE Trans. on Systems, Man, and Cybernetics, Part B: Cybernetics*, 36(1), 96–105. DOI: 10.1109/TSMCB.2005.854502. 32

Anguelov, D., Taskarf, B., Chatalbashev, V., Koller, D., Gupta, D., Heitz, G., and Ng, A. (2005). Discriminative learning of markov random fields for segmentation of 3d scan data. In *Proc. IEEE Conference on Computer Vision and Pattern Recognition*, volume 2, pages 169 – 176 vol. 2. DOI: 10.1109/CVPR.2005.133. 44

Bailly, G., Perrier, P., and Eric Vatikiotis-Bateson, E. (2012). *Audiovisual Speech Processing*. Cambridge University Press. DOI: 10.1017/CBO9780511843891. 70

Baricevic, D., Lee, C., Turk, M., Hollerer, T., and Bowman, D. (2012). A hand-held ar magic lens with user-perspective rendering. In *2012 IEEE International Symposium on Mixed and Augmented Reality (ISMAR)*, pages 197–206. DOI: 10.1109/ISMAR.2012.6402557. 78

Bartlett, M. S., Donato, G., Movellan, J., Hager, J., Ekman, P., and Sejnowski, T. J. (2000). Image representations for facial expression coding. *Advances in neural information processing systems*, **12**, 886–892. 82

Bebis, G., Gyaourova, A., Singh, S., and Pavlidis, I. (2006). Face recognition by fusing thermal infrared and visible imagery. *Image and Vision Computing*, **24**(7), 727–742. DOI: 10.1016/j.imavis.2006.01.017. 71

Belhumeur, P. N., Hespanha, J. P., and Kriegman, D. J. (1997). Eigenfaces vs. Fisherfaces: Recognition using class specific linear projection. *IEEE Trans. Pattern Anal. Mach. Intelligence*, **19**(7), 711–720. Special Issue on Face Recognition. DOI: 10.1109/34.598228. 16, 17, 18

Belhumeur, P. N., Chen, D., Feiner, S., Jacobs, D. W., Kress, W. J., Ling, H., Lopez, I., Ramamoorthi, R., Sheorey, S., White, S., and Zhang, L. (2008). Searching the world's herbaria: A system for visual identification of plant species. In *Proc. European Conf. on Computer Vision*, volume 4, pages 116–129. DOI: 10.1007/978-3-540-88693-8_9. 12

Belhumeur, P. N., Jacobs, D. W., Kriegman, D. J., and Kumar, N. (2011). Localizing parts of faces using a consensus of exemplars. In *Proc. IEEE Conference on Computer Vision and Pattern Recognition*, pages 545–552. DOI: 10.1109/CVPR.2011.5995602. 35, 37

Belongie, S., Malik, J., and Puzicha, J. (2002). Shape matching and object recognition using shape contexts. *IEEE Transactions on Pattern Analysis and Machine Intelligence*, **24**(4), 509–522. DOI: 10.1109/34.993558. 40

Beymer, D. and Flickner, M. (2003). Eye gaze tracking using an active stereo head. In *Proc. IEEE Conference on Computer Vision and Pattern Recognition*, volume 2, pages 451–4588. DOI: 10.1109/CVPR.2003.1211502. 38

Bledsoe, W. W. (1966). Man-machine facial recognition. Technical report, Panoramic Research Inc., Palo Alto, CA. 4

Bobick, A., Davis, J., and Intille, S. (1997). The kidsroom: an example application using a deep perceptual interface. In *Proc. Workshop on Perceptual User Interfaces*, pages 1–4. 6

Bobick, A. F. (1997). Movement, activity, and action: The role of knowledge in the perception of motion. *Royal Society Workshop on Knowledge-based Vision in Man and Machine*, **352**, 1257–1265. DOI: 10.1098/rstb.1997.0108. 3

Bolt, R. A. (1980). "put-that-there": Voice and gesture at the graphics interface. In *ACM Computer Graphics*, volume 14:3. ACM. DOI: 10.1145/965105.807503. 6, 67, 68

Borges, P., Conci, N., and Cavallaro, A. (2013). Video-based human behavior understanding: a survey. *Circuits and Systems for Video Technology, IEEE Transactions on*, **PP**(99), 1–1. DOI: 10.1109/TCSVT.2013.2270402. 76

Bourdev, L. and Malik, J. (2009). Poselets: Body part detectors trained using 3d human pose annotations. In *Proc. IEEE International Conference on Computer Vision*, pages 1365 –1372. DOI: 10.1109/ICCV.2009.5459303. 44

Bradski, G. R. (1998). Real time face and object tracking as a component of a perceptual user interface. In *Proceedings of the 4th IEEE Workshop on Applications of Computer Vision (WACV'98)*, WACV '98, pages 214–, Washington, DC, USA. IEEE Computer Society. DOI: 10.1109/ACV.1998.732882. 52

Bregler, C. and Malik, J. (1998). Tracking people with twists and exponential maps. In *Proc. IEEEConference on Computer Vision and Pattern Recognition*, pages 8 –15. DOI: 10.1109/CVPR.1998.698581. 43

Bretzner, L., Laptev, I., and Lindeberg, T. (2002). Hand gesture recognition using multi-scale colour features, hierarchical models and particle filtering. In *Automatic Face and Gesture Recognition, 2002. Proceedings. Fifth IEEE International Conference on*, pages 423 –428. DOI: 10.1109/AFGR.2002.1004190. 52, 55

Buddharaju, P., Pavlidis, I., Tsiamyrtzis, P., and Bazakos, M. (2007). Physiology-based face recognition in the thermal infrared spectrum. *IEEE Transactions on Pattern Analysis and Machine Intelligence*, **29**(4), 613–626. DOI: 10.1109/TPAMI.2007.1007. 71

Buehler, P., Everingham, M., Huttenlocher, D. P., and Zisserman, A. (2008). Long term arm and hand tracking for continuous sign language tv broadcasts. In *British Machine Vision Conference*. 39

Burt, P. J. (1988). Smart sensing within a pyramid vision machine. *Proceedings of the IEEE*, **76**(8), 1006–1015. DOI: 10.1109/5.5971. 4

Canada, C., Gorodnichy, D. O., Malik, S., and Roth, G. (2002). Nouse "use your nose as a mouse" - a new technology for hands-free games and interfaces. In *Proc. Vision Interface*, pages 354–361. 52

Cao, X. and Wipf, D. (2013). A practical transfer learning algorithm for face verification. In *Proc. IEEE International Conference on Computer Vision*, Sydney, Australia. 18

Cao, X., Wei, Y., Wen, F., and Sun, J. (2012). Face alignment by explicit shape regression. In *CVPR*, pages 2887–2894. DOI: 10.1109/CVPR.2012.6248015. 37

Chang, C.-C. and Lin, C.-J. (2011). LIBSVM: A library for support vector machines. *ACM Transactions on Intelligent Systems and Technology*, **2**, 27:1–27:27. Software available at http://www.csie.ntu.edu.tw/~cjlin/libsvm. DOI: 10.1145/1961189.1961199. 25

Chang, Y., Vieira, M., Turk, M., and Velho, L. (2005). Automatic 3d facial expression analysis in videos. analysis and modelling of faces and gestures. In *Proc. IEEE International Workshop Analysis and Modeling of Faces and Gestures*, volume 3723, pages 293–307. DOI: 10.1007/11564386_23. 32

Chang, Y., Hu, C., Feris, R., and Turk, M. (2006). Manifold based analysis of facial expression. *Image Vision Computing*, **24**, 605–614. DOI: 10.1016/j.imavis.2005.08.006. 32

Chau, M. and Betke, M. (2005). Real time eye tracking and blink detection with usb cameras. Technical Report 2005-12, Boston University. 54

Chaudhry, R., Ravichandran, A., Hager, G., and Vidal, R. (2009). Histograms of oriented optical flow and binet-cauchy kernels on nonlinear dynamical systems for the recognition of human actions. In *Proc. IEEEConference on Computer Vision and Pattern Recognition*, pages 1932–1939. DOI: 10.1109/CVPR.2009.5206821. 56

Chen, D., Cao, X., Wang, L., Wen, F., and Sun, J. (2012). Bayesian face revisited: A joint formulation. In *Proc. European Conf. on Computer Vision*, volume 7534. Springer. DOI: 10.1007/978-3-642-33712-3_41. 27

Chen, D., Cao, X., Wen, F., and Sun, J. (2013). Fusing robust face region descriptors via multiple metric learning for face recognition in the wild. In *Proc. IEEE Conf. on Computer Vision and Pattern Recognition*, Portland, OR. 16, 19, 30

Chen, F. S., Fu, C. M., and Huang, C. L. (2003a). Hand gesture recognition using a real-time tracking method and hidden markov models. *Image and Vision Computing*, **21**, 745–758. DOI: 10.1016/S0262-8856(03)00070-2. 60

Chen, J. and Ji, Q. (2011). Probabilistic gaze estimation without active personal calibration. In *Proc. IEEE Conference on Computer Vision and Pattern Recognition*, Colorado Springs, CO. DOI: 10.1109/CVPR.2011.5995675. 14, 37, 38, 39

Chen, J., Tong, Y., Gray, W., and Ji, Q. (2008). A robust 3d eye gaze tracking system using noise reduction. In *Proc. of The Symposium on Eye Tracking Research & applications*, pages 189–196. DOI: 10.1145/1344471.1344518. 38

Chen, X., Flynn, P. J., and Bowyer, K. (2003b). Visible-light and infrared face recognition. In *Workshop on Multimodal User Authentication*. 71

Chen, Y., Baran, M., Sundaram, H., and Rikakis, T. (2011). A low cost, adaptive mixed reality system for home-based stroke rehabilitation. In *Engineering in Medicine and Biology
Society,EMBC, 2011 Annual International Conference of the IEEE*, pages 1827–1830. DOI:
10.1109/IEMBS.2011.6090520. 75

Coen, M. H. (2001). Multimodal integration – a biological view. In *International Joint Conference
on Artificial Intelligence*, pages 1417–1424. Lawrence Erlbaum Associates. 69

Cohen, I., Sebe, N., Garg, A., Chen, L. S., and Huang, T. S. (2003). Facial expression recognition from video sequences: temporal and static modeling. *Computer Vision and Image Understanding*, **91**(1-2), 160 – 187. <ce:title>Special Issue on Face Recognition</ce:title>. DOI:
10.1016/S1077-3142(03)00081-X. 32

Cohn, J. F., Reed, L. I., Ambadar, Z., Xiao, J., and Moriyama, T. (2004). Automatic analysis and
recognition of brow actions and head motion in spontaneous facial behavior. In *IEEE International Conf. on Systems, Man and Cybernetics*, volume 1, pages 610–616. DOI: 10.1109/IC-
SMC.2004.1398367. 32, 33

Cootes, T. and C.J.Taylor (1992). Active shape models - smart snakes. In *In British Machine
Vision Conference*, pages 266–275. Springer-Verlag. DOI: 10.1007/978-1-4471-3201-1_28.
40

Cootes, T. F., Edwards, G. J., and Taylor, C. J. (2001). Active appearance models. *IEEE Transactions on Pattern Analysis and Machine Intelligence*, **23**(6), 681–685. DOI: 10.1109/34.927467.
32, 34

Cui, Z., Li, W., Xu, D., Shan, S., and Chen, X. (2013). Fusing robust face region descriptors
via multiple metric learning for face recognition in the wild. In *Proc. IEEE Conf. on Computer
Vision and Pattern Recognition*, Portland, OR. 16, 19, 30

Dalal, N. and Triggs, B. (2005). Histograms of oriented gradients for human detection. In *Proc.
IEEEConference on Computer Vision and Pattern Recognition*. DOI: 10.1109/CVPR.2005.177.
42, 43

Darrell, T. and Pentland, A. (1993). Space-time gestures. In *Computer Vision and Pattern Recognition, 1993. Proceedings CVPR'93., 1993 IEEE Computer Society Conference on*, pages 335–340.
IEEE. DOI: 10.1109/CVPR.1993.341109. 6

Davis, J. and Shah, M. (1994). Recognizing hand gestures. In *Proc. European Conference on
Computer Vision*. DOI: 10.1007/3-540-57956-7_37. 55

Davis, J. W. and Bobick, A. F. (1997). The representation and recognition of human
movement using temporal templates. In *Computer Vision and Pattern Recognition, 1997.
Proceedings., 1997 IEEE Computer Society Conference on*, pages 928–934. IEEE. DOI:
10.1109/CVPR.1997.609439. 6

De la Torre, F. and Cohn, J. F. (2011). *Guide to Visual Analysis of Humans: Looking at People*, chapter Facial Expression Analysis. Springer. 32

Dias, J., Vinzce, M., Corke, P., and Lobo, J. (2007). Editorial special issue: 2nd workshop on integration of vision and inertial sensors. *The International Journal of Robotics Research*, **26**(6), 515–517. DOI: 10.1177/0278364907079903. 72

Dixit, M., Rasiwasia, N., and Vasconcelos, N. (2011). Adapted gaussian models for image classification. In *Computer Vision and Pattern Recognition (CVPR), 2011 IEEE Conference on*, pages 937 –943. DOI: 10.1109/CVPR.2011.5995674. 25

Dollar, P., Babenko, B., Belongie, S., Perona, P., and Tu, Z. (2008). Multiple component learning for object detection. Proc. European Conference on Computer Vision. 42, 43

D'Orazio, T., Leo, M., Cicirelli, G., and Distante, A. (2004). An algorithm for real time eye detection in face images. In *International Conference on Pattern Recognition*, volume 3, pages 278–281. DOI: 10.1109/ICPR.2004.148. 36

Dornaika, F. and Raducanu, B. (2008). Facial expression recognition for hci applications. *Encyclopedia of Artficial Intelligence, IGI Global*, **2**, 625–631. DOI: 10.4018/978-1-59904-849-9.ch095. 13

Dumas, B., Lalanne, D., and Oviatt, S. (2009). Multimodal interfaces: A survey of principles, models and frameworks. In *Human Machine Interaction*, pages 3–26. Springer. DOI: 10.1007/978-3-642-00437-7_1. 69

Efthimiou, E., Fotinea, S.-E., Vogler, C., Hanke, T., Glauert, J. R. W., Bowden, R., Braffort, A., Collet, C., Maragos, P., and Segouat, J. (2009). Sign language recognition, generation, and modelling: A research effort with applications in deaf communication. In *HCI (5)*, pages 21–30. DOI: 10.1007/978-3-642-02707-9_3. 62

Ekman, P. (2005). *Emotion in the Human Face*. Oxford University Press. 14

Ekman, P. and Friesen, W. V. (1978). *Facial Action Coding System: A Technique for the Measurement of Facial Movement*. Consulting Psychologists Press, Palo Alto. 31, 53

Elgammal, A., Shet, V., Yacoob, Y., and Davis, L. S. (2003). Learning dynamics for exemplar-based gesture recognition. In *Proc. IEEE Conference on Computer Vision and Pattern Recognition*. 55, 56, 58, 59

Essa, I. A. and Pentland, A. P. (1997). Coding, analysis, interpretation, and recognition of facial expressions. *Pattern Analysis and Machine Intelligence, IEEE Transactions on*, **19**(7), 757–763. DOI: 10.1109/34.598232. 6

Essig, K., Dornbusch, D., Prinzhorn, D., Ritter, H., Maycock, J., and Schack, T. (2012). Automatic analysis of 3d gaze coordinates on scene objects using data from eye-tracking and motion-capture systems. In *Proceedings of the Symposium on Eye Tracking Research and Applications*, ETRA '12, pages 37–44, New York, NY, USA. ACM. DOI: 10.1145/2168556.2168561. 72

Felzenszwalb, P., Girshick, R., and McAllester, D. (2010a). Cascade object detection with deformable part models. In *Proc. IEEEConference on Computer Vision and Pattern Recognition*, pages 2241 –2248. 42, 43

Felzenszwalb, P., Girshick, R., McAllester, D., and Ramanan, D. (2010b). Object detection with discriminatively trained part-based models. *Pattern Analysis and Machine Intelligence, IEEE Transactions on*, **32**(9), 1627 –1645. DOI: 10.1109/TPAMI.2009.167. 42, 43

Felzenszwalb, P. F. and Huttenlocher, D. P. (2005). Pictorial structures for object recognition. *Int. J. Comput. Vision*, **61**, 55–79. DOI: 10.1023/B:VISI.0000042934.15159.49. 43

Felzenszwalb, P. F., McAllester, D., and Ramanan, D. (2008). A discriminatively trained, multiscale, deformable part model. Proc. IEEEConference on Computer Vision and Pattern Recognition. 42, 43

Feris, R. S., Gemmell, J., Toyama, K., and Krüger, V. (2002). Hierarchical wavelet networks for facial feature localization. In *Proc. IEEE Conference on Face and Gesture Recognition*. DOI: 10.1109/AFGR.2002.1004143. 36

Fleming, M. K. and Cottrell, G. W. (1990). Categorization of faces using unsupervised feature extraction. In *IJCNN International Joint Conference on Neural Networks*, pages 65–70. IEEE. DOI: 10.1109/IJCNN.1990.137696. 4

Flórez, F., García, J. M., García, J., and Hernández, A. (2002). Hand gesture recognition following the dynamics of a topology-preserving network. In *Proc. IEEE Conference on Face and Gesture Recognition*. DOI: 10.1109/AFGR.2002.1004173. 55

Forssen, P. and Lowe, D. (2007). Shape descriptors for maximally stable extremal regions. In *Proc. IEEE International Conference on Computer Vision*. DOI: 10.1109/ICCV.2007.4409025. 61

Freeman, W. T. and Roth, M. (1995). Orientation histograms for hand gesture recognition. In *Proc. IEEE Conference on Face and Gesture Recognition*. 40, 56

Freeman, W. T. and Weissman, C. D. (1995). Television control by hand gestures. In *IEEE Intl. Wkshp. on Automatic Face and Gesture Recognition*, Zurich. 48, 49, 50, 52

Fu, Y. and Huang, T. S. (2007). hmouse: Head tracking driven virtual computer mouse. In *Proceedings of the Eighth IEEE Workshop on Applications of Computer Vision*, WACV '07, pages 30–, Washington, DC, USA. IEEE Computer Society. DOI: 10.1109/WACV.2007.29. 52

Fu, Y. and Huang, T. S. (2008). Human age estimation with regression on discriminative aging manifold. *Multimedia, IEEE Transactions on*, **10**(4), 578–584. DOI: 10.1109/TMM.2008.921847. 34

Fu, Y., Guo, G., and Huang, T. S. (2010). Age synthesis and estimation via faces: A survey. *Pattern Analysis and Machine Intelligence, IEEE Transactions on*, **32**(11), 1955–1976. DOI: 10.1109/TPAMI.2010.36. 33

Gan, L. and Liu, Q. (2010). Eye detection based on rank order filter and projection function. In *International Conf. on Computer Design and Applications*, volume 1, pages V1–642 –V1–645. DOI: 10.1109/ICCDA.2010.5540901. 36

Gao, W., Fang, G., Zhao, D., and Chen, Y. (2004). A chinese sign language recognition system based on sofm/srn/hmm. *Pattern Recogn.*, **37**(12), 2389–2402. DOI: 10.1016/j.patcog.2004.04.008. 62

Gauvain, J.-L. and Lee, C.-H. (1994). Maximum a posteriori estimation for multivariate gaussian mixture observations of markov chains. *IEEE Transactions on Speech and Audio Processing*, **2**(2), 291–298. DOI: 10.1109/89.279278. 22, 25

Geng, X., Zhou, Z.-H., Zhang, Y., Li, G., and Dai, H. (2006). Learning from facial aging patterns for automatic age estimation. In *Proc. The 14th Annual ACM International Conference on Multimedia*, pages 307–316. DOI: 10.1145/1180639.1180711. 34

Geng, X., Zhou, Z.-H., and Smith-Miles, K. (2007). Automatic age estimation based on facial aging patterns. *IEEE Transactions on Pattern Analysis and Machine Intelligence*, **29**(12), 2234–2240. DOI: 10.1109/TPAMI.2007.70733. 34

Georghiades, A. S., Belhumeur, P. N., and Kriegman, D. J. (2001). From few to many: Illumination cone models for face recognition under variable lighting and pose. *IEEE Trans. Pattern Anal. Mach. Intelligence*, **23**(6), 643–660. DOI: 10.1109/34.927464. 16, 17, 18

Goldberg, J. H. and Kotval, X. P. (1999). Computer interface evaluation using eye movements: methods and constructs. *International Journal of Industrial Ergonomics*, **24**(6), 631 – 645. DOI: 10.1016/S0169-8141(98)00068-7. 54

Goodrich, M. and Schultz, A. (2007). Human–robot interaction: A survey. *Foundations and Trends in Human-Computer Interaction*, **1**(3), 203–275. DOI: 10.1561/1100000005. 76

Grest, D., Woetzel, J., and Koch, R. (2005). Nonlinear body pose estimation from depth images. In *Proc. 27th Annual meeting of the German Association for Pattern Recognition*, pages 285–292, Vienna, Austria. DOI: 10.1007/11550518_36. 44

Gross, R., Matthews, I., Cohn, J. F., Kanade, T., and Baker, S. (2010). Multi-pie. *Image Vision Computing*, **28**(5), 807–813. DOI: 10.1016/j.imavis.2009.08.002. 17

Gu, L. and Kanade, T. (2008). A generative shape regularization model for robust face alignment. In *Proc. European Conference on Computer Vision*, pages 413–426. DOI: 10.1007/978-3-540-88682-2_32. 37

Guestrin, E. D. and Eizenman, M. (2006). General theory of remote gaze estimation using the pupil center and corneal reflections. *IEEE Transactions on Biomedical Engineering*, **53**(6), 1124–1133. DOI: 10.1109/TBME.2005.863952. 38

Guestrin, E. D. and Eizenman, M. (2008). Remote point-of-gaze estimation requiring a single-point calibration for applications with infants. In *Proc. the symposium on Eye tracking research & applications*, pages 267–274. DOI: 10.1145/1344471.1344531. 38

Gunay, A. and Nabiyev, V. V. (2007). Automatic detection of anthropometric features from facial images. In *IEEE Conf. on Signal Processing and Communications Applications*. DOI: 10.1109/SIU.2007.4298656. 33, 34

Guo, G. and Dyer, C. R. (2005). Learning from examples in the small sample case: face expression recognition. *IEEE Trans. on Systems, Man, and Cybernetics, Part B: Cybernetics*, **35**(3), 477–488. DOI: 10.1109/TSMCB.2005.846658. 32

Guo, G., Fu, Y., Dyer, C. R., and Huang, T. S. (2008). Image-based human age estimation by manifold learning and locally adjusted robust regression. *IEEE Trans. on Image Processing*, **17**(7), 1178–1188. DOI: 10.1109/TIP.2008.924280. 34, 35

Guo, G., Mu, G., Fu, Y., and Huang, T. S. (2009). Human age estimation using bio-inspired features. In *Proc. IEEE Conference on Computer Vision and Pattern Recognition*, pages 112–119. DOI: 10.1109/CVPR.2009.5206681. 34, 35

Guyon, I., Athitsos, V., Jangyodsuk, P., Hamner, B., and Escalante, H. (2012). Chalearn gesture challenge: Design and first results. In *Computer Vision and Pattern Recognition Workshops (CVPRW), 2012 IEEE Computer Society Conference on*, pages 1–6. DOI: 10.1109/CVPRW.2012.6239178. 41

Hansen, D. W. and Ji, Q. (2010). In the eye of the beholder: A survey of models for eyes and gaze. *IEEE Trans. on Pattern Analysis and Machine Intelligence*, **32**(3), 478–500. DOI: 10.1109/TPAMI.2009.30. 14

Harel, J., Koch, C., and Perona, P. (2007). Graph-based visual saliency. In *Proc. Neural Information Processing Systems*, pages 545–552. MIT Press. 39

Harmon, L., Khan, M., Lasch, R., and Ramig, P. (1981). Machine identification of human faces. *Pattern Recognition*, **13**(2), 97 – 110. DOI: 10.1016/0031-3203(81)90008-X. 4

Haro, A., Flickner, M., and Essa, I. (2000). Detecting and tracking eyes by using their physiological properties, dynamics, and appearance. In *Proc. IEEEConference on Computer Vision and Pattern Recognition*. DOI: 10.1109/CVPR.2000.855815. 35

Hasan, T. and Hansen, J. (2011). A study on universal background model training in speaker verification. *Audio, Speech, and Language Processing, IEEE Transactions on*, **19**(7), 1890 –1899. DOI: 10.1109/TASL.2010.2102753. 21

Hasanuzzaman, M., Ampornaramveth, V., Zhang, T., Bhuiyan, M., Shirai, Y., and Ueno, H. (2004). Real-time vision-based gesture recognition for human robot interaction. In *IEEE International Conference on Robotics and Biomimetics*, pages 413–418. DOI: 10.1109/RO-BIO.2004.1521814. 40

He, X., Yan, S., Hu, Y., Niyogi, P., and Zhang, H. (2005). Face recognition using laplacian-faces. *IEEE Transaction on Pattern Analysis and Machine Intelligence*, **27**(3), 328–340. DOI: 10.1109/TPAMI.2005.55. 16

Hong, P., Turk, M., and Huang, T. S. (2000). Gesture modeling and recognition using finite state machines. In *Proc. IEEE Conference on Face and Gesture Recognition*, pages 410–415. DOI: 10.1109/AFGR.2000.840667. 55

Hua, G. and Akbarzadeh, A. (2009). A robust elastic and partial matching metric for face recognition. In *Proc. of IEEE International Conf. on Computer Vision*, Kyoto, Japan. DOI: 10.1109/ICCV.2009.5459457. 16, 17, 18, 19

Hua, G., Yang, M.-H., and Wu, Y. (2005). Learning to estimate human pose with data driven belief propagation. In *Proc. IEEE Conf. on Computer Vision and Pattern Recognition*, volume 2, pages 747–754. DOI: 10.1109/CVPR.2005.208. 44

Hua, G., Yang, T.-Y., and Vasireddy, S. (2007). Peye: Toward a visual motion based perceptual interface for mobile devices. In *Proc. of IEEE International Workshop on Human Computer Interaction*, pages 39–48, Minneaplois, MN. DOI: 10.1007/978-3-540-75773-3_5. 61, 62

Hua, G., Yang, M.-H., Learned-Miller, E., Ma, Y., Turk, M., Kriegman, D. J., and Huang, T. S. (2011). Introduction to the special section on real-world face recognition. *IEEE Trans. on Pattern Analysis and Machine Intelligence*, **33**(10), 1921–1924. DOI: 10.1109/TPAMI.2011.182. 17

Huang, E.-W. and Fu, L.-C. (2008). Gesture stroke recognition using computer vision and linear accelerometer. In *IEEE International Conference on Automatic Face Gesture Recognition*. DOI: 10.1109/AFGR.2008.4813355. 72

Huang, G., Jain, V., and Learned-Miller, E. (2007a). Unsupervised joint alignment of complex images. In *Computer Vision, 2007. ICCV 2007. IEEE 11th International Conference on*, pages 1 –8. DOI: 10.1109/ICCV.2007.4408858. 28

Huang, G. B., Ramesh, M., Berg, T., and Learned-Miller, E. (2007b). Labeled faces in the wild: a database for studying face recognition in unconstrained environments. Technical Report 07-49, University of Massachusetts, Amherst. 17, 18

Huang, G. B., Mattar, M., Berg, T., and Learned-Miller, E. (2008). Labeled Faces in the Wild: A Database forStudying Face Recognition in Unconstrained Environments. In *Workshop on Faces in 'Real-Life' Images: Detection, Alignment, and Recognition*, Marseille, France. Erik Learned-Miller and Andras Ferencz and Frédéric Jurie. 27, 28

Huang, J. and Wechsler, H. (1999). Eye detection using optimal wavelet packets and radial basis functions (rbfs). *International Journal of Pattern Recognition and Artificial Intelligence*, **13**, 1009–1026. DOI: 10.1142/S0218001499000562. 36

Hummels, C. and Stappers, P. (1998). Meaningful gestures for human computer interaction: beyond hand postures. In *Automatic Face and Gesture Recognition, 1998. Proceedings. Third IEEE International Conference on*, pages 591–596. IEEE. DOI: 10.1109/AFGR.1998.671012. 70

Hutchinson, T., White, K.P., J., Martin, W., Reichert, K., and Frey, L. (1989). Human-computer interaction using eye-gaze input. *Systems, Man and Cybernetics, IEEE Transactions on*, **19**(6), 1527 –1534. DOI: 10.1109/21.44068. 54

Iannizzotto, G., Costanzo, C., Lanzafame, P., and La Rosa, F. (2005). A vision-based user interface for real-time controlling toy cars. In *Emerging Technologies and Factory Automation, 2005. ETFA 2005. 10th IEEE Conference on*, volume 1, pages 8 pp. –1016. DOI: 10.1109/ETFA.2005.1612634. 48, 49, 50, 51

Ike, T., Kishikawa, N., and Stenger, B. (2007). A real-time hand gesture interface implemented on a multi-core processor. In *IAPR Conference on Machine Vision Applications*, Tokyo, Japan. 52

Ioffe, S. and Forsyth, D. A. (2001). Probabilistic methods for finding people. *International Journal Computer Vision*, **43**, 45–68. DOI: 10.1023/A:1011179004708. 43

Jacob, R. (1993). Hot topics-eye-gaze computer interfaces: what you look at is what you get. *Computer*, **26**(7), 65 –66. DOI: 10.1109/MC.1993.274943. 54

Jacob, R. J. K. (1991). The use of eye movements in human-computer interaction techniques: what you look at is what you get. *ACM Transaction on Information Systems*, **9**, 152–169. DOI: 10.1145/123078.128728. 37, 48, 54

Jaimes, A. and Sebe, N. (2005). Multimodal human computer interaction: A survey. In *Proc. IEEE International Workshop on Human Computer Interaction (in conjunction with ICCV'2005)*, Beijing, China. DOI: 10.1016/j.cviu.2006.10.019. 14

Jaimes, A. and Sebe, N. (2007). Multimodal human–computer interaction: A survey. *Computer vision and image understanding*, **108**(1), 116–134. DOI: 10.1016/j.cviu.2006.10.019. 69

Jesorsky, O., Kirchberg, K. J., and Frischholz, R. (2001). Robust face detection using the hausdorff distance. In *Proc. of the Third International Conference on Audio- and Video-Based Biometric Person Authentication*, pages 90–95, London, UK. Springer-Verlag. DOI: 10.1007/3-540-45344-X_14. 36, 37

Kanade, T. (1973). *Picture Processing System by Computer Complex and Recognition of Human Faces*. Ph.D. thesis, Department of Information Science, Kyoto Univ. 4

Kanda, T. and Ishiguro, H. (2012). *Human–Robot Interaction in Social Robotics*. CRC Press. DOI: 10.1201/b13004. 76

Kang, H., Lee, C. W., and Jung, K. (2004). Recognition-based gesture spotting in video games. *Pattern Recognition Letters*, **25**, 1701–1714. DOI: 10.1016/j.patrec.2004.06.016. 40

Karlinsky, L., Dinerstein, M., Harari, D., and Ullman, S. (2010). The chains model for detecting parts by their context. In *Proc. IEEE Conference on Computer Vision and Pattern Recognition*, pages 25–32. DOI: 10.1109/CVPR.2010.5540232. 39

Kelly, M. D. (1970). Visual identification of people by computer. Technical report, Artificial Intelligence Laboratory, Stanford University. 4

Kim, K.-N. and Ramakrishna, R. (1999). Vision-based eye-gaze tracking for human computer interface. In *Systems, Man, and Cybernetics, 1999. IEEE SMC '99 Conference Proceedings. 1999 IEEE International Conference on*, volume 2, pages 324 –329 vol.2. 54

Kirishima, T., Sato, K., and Chihara, K. (2005). Real-time gesture recognition by learning and selective control of visual interest points. *IEEE Transactions on Pattern Analysis and Machine Intelligence*, **27**, 351–364. DOI: 10.1109/TPAMI.2005.61. 56

Knoop, S., Vacek, S., and Dillmann, R. (2006). Sensor fusion for 3d human body tracking with an articulated 3d body model. In *Proc. IEEE International Conf. on Robotics and Automation*, pages 1686 –1691. DOI: 10.1109/ROBOT.2006.1641949. 44

Kölsch, M. (2004). *Vision Based Hand Gesture Interfaces for Wearable Computing and Virtual Environments*. Ph.D. thesis, University of California, Santa Barbara. 13, 39

Kolsch, M. and Turk, M. (2004a). Fast 2d hand tracking with flocks of features and multi-cue integration. In *Proceedings of the 2004 Conference on Computer Vision and Pattern Recognition Workshop (CVPRW'04) Volume 10 - Volume 10*, CVPRW '04, pages 158–, Washington, DC, USA. IEEE Computer Society. DOI: 10.1109/CVPR.2004.345. 52

Kolsch, M. and Turk, M. (2004b). Robust hand detection. In *Proc. IEEE Conference on Face and Gesture Recognition*, pages 614–619. DOI: 10.1109/AFGR.2004.1301601. 39

Kolsch, M., Turk, M., and Hollerer, T. (2004). Vision-based interfaces for mobility. In *The First Annual International Conference on Mobile and Ubiquitous Systems: Networking and Services, 2004.*, pages 86–94. DOI: 10.1109/MOBIQ.2004.1331713. 39, 40, 41, 75

Kong, S. G., Heo, J., Abidi, B. R., Paik, J., and Abidi, M. A. (2005). Recent advances in visual and infrared face recognition – a review. *Computer Vision and Image Understanding*, **97**, 103–135. DOI: 10.1016/j.cviu.2004.04.001. 71

Kothari, R. and Mitchell, J. L. (1996). Detection of eye locations in unconstrained visual images. In *Image Processing, 1996. Proceedings., International Conference on*, volume 3, pages 519–522. DOI: 10.1109/ICIP.1996.560546. 36

Kumar, M. P., Zisserman, A., and Torr, P. H. (2009). Efficient discriminative learning of parts-based models. In *Proc. IEEE International Conference on Computer Vision*, pages 552–559. DOI: 10.1109/ICCV.2009.5459192. 39

Kumar, R. and Kumar, A. (2008). Black pearl: An alternative for mouse and keyboard. *ICGST International Journal on Graphics, Vision and Image Processing, GVIP*, **08**, 1–6. 52

Kwon, Y. H. and da Vitoria Lobo, N. (1994). Age classification from facial images. In *Proc. IEEE Conference on Computer Vision and Pattern Recognition*, pages 762–767. DOI: 10.1006/cviu.1997.0549. 33, 34

Lafferty, J. D., McCallum, A., and Pereira, F. C. N. (2001). Conditional random fields: Probabilistic models for segmenting and labeling sequence data. In *Proceedings of the Eighteenth International Conference on Machine Learning*, ICML '01, pages 282–289, San Francisco, CA, USA. Morgan Kaufmann Publishers Inc. 59

Lalanne, D., Nigay, L., Robinson, P., Vanderdonckt, J., Ladry, J.-F., *et al.* (2009). Fusion engines for multimodal input: a survey. In *Proceedings of the 2009 international conference on Multimodal interfaces*, pages 153–160. ACM. DOI: 10.1145/1647314.1647343. 69

Lanitis, A., Taylor, C. J., and Cootes, T. F. (2002). Toward automatic simulation of aging effects on face images. *Pattern Analysis and Machine Intelligence, IEEE Transactions on*, **24**(4), 442–455. DOI: 10.1109/34.993553. 34

Lanitis, A., Draganova, C., and Christodoulou, C. (2004). Comparing different classifiers for automatic age estimation. *IEEE Trans. on Systems, Man, and Cybernetics, Part B: Cybernetics*, **34**(1), 621–628. DOI: 10.1109/TSMCB.2003.817091. 34

Laptev, I. (2006). Improvements of object detection using boosted histograms. British Machine Vision Conferences. 43

Lee, T. and Hollerer, T. (2007). Handy ar: Markerless inspection of augmented reality objects using fingertip tracking. In *2007 11th IEEE International Symposium on Wearable Computers*, pages 83–90. DOI: 10.1109/ISWC.2007.4373785. 75

Lehrer, N., Attygalle, S., Wolf, S., and Rikakis, T. (2011a). Exploring the bases for a mixed reality stroke rehabilitation system, part i: A unified approach for representing action, quantitative evaluation, and interactive feedback. *Journal of NeuroEngineering and Rehabilitation*, **8**(1), 51. DOI: 10.1186/1743-0003-8-51. 75

Lehrer, N., Chen, Y., Duff, M., L Wolf, S., and Rikakis, T. (2011b). Exploring the bases for a mixed reality stroke rehabilitation system, part ii: Design of interactive feedback for upper limb rehabilitation. *Journal of NeuroEngineering and Rehabilitation*, **8**(1), 54. DOI: 10.1186/1743-0003-8-54. 75

Li, H., Hua, G., Lin, Z., Brandt, J., and Yang, J. (2013). Probabilistic elastic matching for pose variant face verification. In *Proc. IEEE Conf. on Computer Vision and Pattern Recognition*, Portland, OR. 16, 19, 20, 29, 31

Liang, L., Xiao, R., Wen, F., and Sun, J. (2008). Face alignment via component-based discriminative search. In *Proc. European Conference on Computer Vision*, pages 72–85. DOI: 10.1007/978-3-540-88688-4_6. 37

Lin, Z. and Davis, L. S. (2008). A pose-invariant descriptor for human detection and segmentation. Proc. European Conference on Computer Vision. 42

Lin, Z., Davis, L. S., Doermann, D., and DeMenthon, D. (2007). Hierarchical part-template matching for human detection and segmentation. Proc. IEEE International Conference on Computer Vision. 42

Lin, Z., Hua, G., and Davis, L. S. (2009). Multiple instance feature for robust part-based object detection. In *Proc. of IEEE Conf. on Computer Vision and Pattern Recognition*, Miami Beach, FL. DOI: 10.1109/CVPR.2009.5206858. 42, 43

Litman, D. J. and Forbes-Riley, K. (2004). Predicting student emotions in computer-human tutoring dialogues. In *Proc. The 42nd Annual Meeting on Association for Computational Linguistics*. DOI: 10.3115/1218955.1219000. 32

Liversedge, S. P. and Findlay, J. M. (2000). Saccadic eye movements and cognition. *Trends in Cognitive Sciences*, **4**(1), 6–14. DOI: 10.1016/S1364-6613(99)01418-7. 14

Lockton, R. and Fitzgibbon, A. W. (2002). Real-time gesture recognition using deterministic boosting. In *British Machine Vision Conferences*, pages 817–826. 60

Lucey, S. and Chen, T. (2006). Learning patch dependencies for improved pose mismatched face verification. In *Proc. IEEE Conference on Computer Vision and Pattern Recognition*. DOI: 10.1109/CVPR.2006.172. 16

Lucey, S., Ashraf, A. B., and Cohn, J. F. (2007). Investigating spontaneous facial action recognition through AAM representations of the face. In *Face Recognition, Delac*, pages 275–286. DOI: 10.5772/4841. 32

Ma, Y., Ding, X., Wang, Z., and Wang, N. (2004). Robust precise eye location under probabilistic framework. In *Proc. IEEE Conference on Face and Gesture Recognition*, pages 339–344. DOI: 10.1109/AFGR.2004.1301554. 37

Mace, D., Gao, W., and Coskun, A. K. (2013). Improving accuracy and practicality of accelerometer-based hand gesture recognition. In *IUI 2013 Workshop on Interacting with Smart Objects*. 72

Maji, S., Berg, A. C., and Malik, J. (2008). Classification using intersection kernel support vector machines is efficient. Proc. IEEE Conference on Computer Vision and Pattern Recognition. 42

Marcel, S., Bernier, O., and Collobert, D. (2000). Hand gesture recognition using input-output hidden markov models. In *Proc. IEEE Conference on Face and Gesture Recognition*. DOI: 10.1109/AFGR.2000.840674. 55, 56

Martin1, C. S., Carrillo, R., Meza, P., Mendez-Vazquez, H., Plasencia, Y., García-Reyes, E., and Hermosilla, G. (2011). Recent advances on face recognition using thermal infrared images. In P. M. Corcoran, editor, *Reviews, Refinements and New Ideas in Face Recognition*, pages 95–112. InTech. DOI: 10.5772/743. 71

Mason, M. F., Hood, B. M., and Macrae, C. N. (2004). Look into my eyes: Gaze direction and person memory. *Memory*, **12**(5), 637–643. DOI: 10.1080/09658210344000152. 14

Matas, J., Chum, O., Urban, M., and Pajdla, T. (2002). Robust wide baseline stereo from maximally stable extremal regions. In *British Machine Vision Conferences*. 61

McGurk, H. and MacDonald, J. (1976).   Hearing lips and seeing voices.   *Nature*. DOI: 10.1038/264746a0. 70

McNeill, D. (1992). *Hand and mind: What gestures reveal about thought*. University of Chicago Press. 69

Mendez-Vazquez, H., Martinez-Diaz, Y., and Chai, Z. (2013). Volume structured ordinal features with background similarity measure for video face recognition. 30, 31

Microsoft (2010). Kinect adventures!–explore the world and beyond! 48, 49, 52

Mikolajczyk, K., Schmid, C., and Zisserman, A. (2004). Human detection based on a probabilistic assembly of robust part detectors. Proc. European Conference on Computer Vision. 42

Mitra, S. and Acharya, T. (2007a).   Gesture recognition: A survey.   *Systems, Man, and Cybernetics, Part C: Applications and Reviews, IEEE Transactions on*, **37**(3), 311–324. DOI: 10.1109/TSMCC.2007.893280. 42

Mitra, S. and Acharya, T. (2007b). Gesture recognition: A survey. *IEEE Trans. on Systems, Man and Cybernetics - Part C*, **37**(3), 311–324. DOI: 10.1109/TSMCC.2007.893280. 55

Mittal, A., Zisserman, A., and Torr, P. H. S. (2011). Hand detection using multiple proposals. In *British Machine Vision Conference*. DOI: 10.5244/C.25.75. 39, 40

Moghaddam, B., Jebara, T., and Pentland, A. (2000). Bayesian face recognition. *Pattern Recognition*, **33**(11), 1771–1782. DOI: 10.1016/S0031-3203(99)00179-X. 16

Mori, G. and Malik, J. (2002).   Estimating human body configurations using shape context matching. In *Proceedings of the 7th European Conference on Computer Vision-Part III*, ECCV '02, pages 666–680, London, UK, UK. Springer-Verlag. DOI: 10.1007/3-540-47977-5_44. 44

Morimoto, C. H., Amir, A., and Flickner, M. (2002). Detecting eye position and gaze from a single camera and 2 light sources. In *Proc. The 16th International Conference on Pattern Recognition*, volume 4, pages 314–317. DOI: 10.1109/ICPR.2002.1047459. 37

Nicolaou, M. A., Gunes, H., and Pantic, M. (2011).   Output-associative rvm regression for dimensional and continuous emotion prediction. In *Proc. IEEE Conference on Face and Gesture Recognition*, Santa Barbara, CA. DOI: 10.1109/FG.2011.5771396. 33

Nicolle, J., Rapp, V., Bailly, K., Prevost, L., and Chetouani, M. (2012). Robust continuous prediction of human emotions using multiscale dynamic cues. In *2nd International Audio/Visual Emotion Challenge and Workshop*, AVEC 2012, pages 501–508, New York, NY, USA. ACM. DOI: 10.1145/2388676.2388783. 70

Ning, H., Han, T. X., Hu, Y., Zhang, Z., Fu, Y., and Huang, T. S. (2006). A realtime shrug detector. In *Proc. The 7th IEEE International Conf. on Automatic Face and Gesture REcognition*, Southampton, UK. DOI: 10.1109/FGR.2006.15. 14

Nistér, D. and Stewénius, H. (2006). Scalable recognition with a vocabulary tree. In *Proc. IEEEConference on Computer Vision and Pattern Recognition*, pages 2161–2168. DOI: 10.1109/CVPR.2006.264. 61

Nowak, E. and Jurie, F. (2007). Learning visual similarity measures for comparing never seen objects. In *Proc. of IEEE Conf. on Computer Vision and Pattern Recognition*, Minneapolis, MN. DOI: 10.1109/CVPR.2007.382969. 29

Oliva, A. and Torralba, A. (2001). Modeling the shape of the scene: a holistic representation of the spatial envelope. *International Journal of Computer Vision*, **42**(3), 145–175. DOI: 10.1023/A:1011139631724. 12

Ong, E.-J. and Bowden, R. (2004). A boosted classifier tree for hand shape detection. In *Proc. IEEE Conference on Face and Gesture Recognition*, pages 889–894. DOI: 10.1109/AFGR.2004.1301646. 39

Oviatt, S. and Cohen, P. (2000). Perceptual user interfaces: multimodal interfaces that process what comes naturally. *Communications of the ACM*, **43**(3), 45–53. DOI: 10.1145/330534.330538. 6

Oviatt, S., Cohen, P., Wu, L., Duncan, L., Suhm, B., Bers, J., Holzman, T., Winograd, T., Landay, J., Larson, J., *et al.* (2000). Designing the user interface for multimodal speech and pen-based gesture applications: state-of-the-art systems and future research directions. *Human-computer interaction*, **15**(4), 263–322. DOI: 10.1207/S15327051HCI1504_1. 67

Oviatt, S., Lunsford, R., and Coulston, R. (2005). Individual differences in multimodal integration patterns: What are they and why do they exist? In *Proceedings of the SIGCHI Conference on Human Factors in Computing Systems (CHI 2005)*, pages 241–249. ACM. DOI: 10.1145/1054972.1055006. 67

Pang, J., Huang, Q., and Jiang, S. (2008). Multiple instance boost using graph embedding based decision stump for pedestrian detection. Proc. European Conference on Computer Vision. 43

Pantic, M. and Bartlett, M. S. (2007). Machine analysis of facial expressions. In K. Delac and M. Grgic, editors, *Face Recognition*, pages 377–416. I-Tech Education and Publishing, Vienna, Austria. DOI: 10.5772/38. 32

Pantic, M. and Rothkrantz, L. J. M. (2000). Automatic analysis of facial expressions: The state of the art. *IEEE Transactions on Pattern Analysis and Machine Intelligence*, **22**(12), 1424–1445. DOI: 10.1109/34.895976. 14

Pantic, M., Pentland, A., Nijholt, A., and Huang, T. S. (2007). Human computing and machine understanding of human behavior: a survey. In *Artifical Intelligence for Human Computing*, pages 47–71. Springer. DOI: 10.1007/978-3-540-72348-6_3. 76

Papageorgiou, C., Oren, M., and Poggio, T. (1998a). A general framework for object detection. In *Proc. IEEE International Conference on Computer Vision*, pages 555–562. DOI: 10.1109/ICCV.1998.710772. 15

Papageorgiou, C., Evgeniou, T., and Poggio, T. (1998b). A trainable pedestrian detection system. In *In Proc. of Intelligent Vehicles*. 42

Paucher, R. and Turk, M. (2010). Location-based augmented reality on mobile phones. In *Workshop on Mobile Computer Vision*, pages 9–16. IEEE. DOI: 10.1109/CVPRW.2010.5543249. 72

Pavlovic, V., Sharma, R., and Huang, T. (1997). Visual interpretation of hand gestures for human-computer interaction: a review. *Pattern Analysis and Machine Intelligence, IEEE Transactions on*, 19(7), 677–695. DOI: 10.1109/34.598226. 48

Pentland, A. (2000). Looking at people: sensing for ubiquitous and wearable computing. *IEEE Transactions on Pattern Analysis and Machine Intelligence*, 22(1). DOI: 10.1109/34.824823. 1

Pentland, A., Moghaddam, B., and Starner, T. (1994). View-based and modular eigenspaces for face recognition. In *Computer Vision and Pattern Recognition, 1994. Proceedings CVPR'94., 1994 IEEE Computer Society Conference on*, pages 84–91. IEEE. DOI: 10.1109/CVPR.1994.323814. 6

Petajan, E. (1984). *Automatic lipreading to enhance speech recognition*. Phd dissertation, University of Illinois at Urbana-Champaign. 70

Philips, P. J., Moon, H., Rizvi, S. A., and Rauss, P. J. (2000). The feret evaluation methodology for face recognition algorithms. *IEEE Transactions on Pattern Analysis and Machine Intelligence*, 22(10), 1090–1103. DOI: 10.1109/34.879790. 17

Phillips, P. J., Flynn, P. J., Scruggs, T., Bowyer, K. W., Chang, J., Hoffman, K., Marques, J., Min, J., and Worek, W. (2005). Overview of the face recognition grand challenge. In *Proc. IEEE Conference on Computer Vision and Pattern Recognition*, pages 947–954, Washington, DC, USA. IEEE Computer Society. DOI: 10.1109/CVPR.2005.268. 17

Picard, R. W. (1997). *Affective Computing*. MIT Press. 14

Picard, R. W. (1999). Affective computing for hci. In *Proc. of The 8th International Conference on Human-Computer Interaction: Ergonomics and User Interfaces*, volume 1, pages 829–833, Hillsdale, NJ, USA. 13

Pinto, N., DiCarlo, J. J., and Cox, D. D. (2009). How far can you get with a modern face recognition test set using only simple features? In *IEEE Computer Vision and Pattern Recognition*. 27, 29

Plagemann, C., Ganapathi, V., Koller, D., and Thrun, S. (2010). Real-time identification and localization of body parts from depth images. In *IEEE International Conference on Robotics and Automation*, pages 3108 –3113. DOI: 10.1109/ROBOT.2010.5509559. 44

Poppe, R. (2007). Vision-based human motion analysis: An overview. *Comput. Vis. Image Underst.*, **108**, 4–18. DOI: 10.1016/j.cviu.2006.10.016. 43

Potamianos, G., Neti, C., Luettin, J., and Matthews, I. (2004). Audio-visual automatic speech recognition: An overview. *Issues in Visual and Audio-Visual Speech Processing*, **22**, 23. 70

Quek, F., McNeill, D., Bryll, R., Duncan, S., Ma, X.-F., Kirbas, C., McCullough, K. E., and Ansari, R. (2002). Multimodal human discourse: gesture and speech. *ACM Transactions on Computer-Human Interaction*, **9**(3), 171–193. DOI: 10.1145/568513.568514. 82

Rabiner, L. R. (1979). A tutorial on hidden markov models and selected applications in speech recognition. *Proc. of IEEE*, **77**(2), 257–286. DOI: 10.1109/5.18626. 62, 64

Rajko, S., Qian, G., Ingalls, T., and James, J. (2007). Real-time gesture recognition with minimal training requirements and on-line learning. In *Proc. IEEE Conference on Computer Vision and Pattern Recognition*. DOI: 10.1109/CVPR.2007.383330. 55, 56, 57

Ramanan, D., Forsyth, D., and Zisserman, A. (2005). Strike a pose: tracking people by finding stylized poses. In *Computer Vision and Pattern Recognition, 2005. CVPR 2005. IEEE Computer Society Conference on*, volume 1, pages 271 – 278 vol. 1. DOI: 10.1109/CVPR.2005.335. 44

Ramanathan, N. and Chellappa, R. (2006). Modeling age progression in young faces. In *Proc. IEEE Conference on Computer Vision and Pattern Recognition*, volume 1, pages 387–394. DOI: 10.1109/CVPR.2006.187. 33, 34 .

Raskar, R., Welch, G., Cutts, M., Lake, A., Stesin, L., and Fuchs, H. (1998). The office of the future: a unified approach to image-based modeling and spatially immersive displays. In *Proc. of the 25th annual conference on Computer graphics and interactive techniques*, SIGGRAPH '98, pages 179–188, New York, NY, USA. ACM. DOI: 10.1145/280814.280861. 40

Rauschert, I., Agrawal, P., Sharma, R., Fuhrmann, S., Brewer, I., and MacEachren, A. (2002). Designing a human-centered, multimodal gis interface to support emergency management. In *Proceedings of the 10th ACM international symposium on Advances in geographic information systems*, GIS '02, pages 119–124, New York, NY, USA. ACM. DOI: 10.1145/585147.585172. 40

Roberts, L. G. (1963). *Machine perception of three-dimensional solids*. Phd dissertation, Department of Electrical Engineering, MIT. 1

Robertson, P., Laddaga, R., and Van Kleek, M. (2004). Virtual mouse vision based interface. In *Proceedings of the 9th international conference on Intelligent user interfaces*, IUI '04, pages 177–183, New York, NY, USA. ACM. DOI: 10.1145/964442.964476. 52

Rogalla, ., Ehrenmann, M., Zollner, R., Becher, R., and Dillmann, R. (2002). Using gesture and speech control for commanding a robot assistant. In *Proc. 11th IEEE International Workshop on Robot and Human Interactive Communication*, pages 454–459. DOI: 10.1109/RO-MAN.2002.1045664. 40

Rowley, H. A., Baluja, S., and Kanade, T. (1998). Neural network-based face detection. *IEEE Trans. on Pattern Analysis Machine Intelligence*, **20**(1), 23–38. DOI: 10.1109/34.655647. 15

Sachez-Nielsen, E., Anton-Canals, L., and Herndez-Tejera, M. (2004). Hand gesture recognition for human-machine interaction. In *Journal of WSCG*, pages 395–402. 48, 49, 51

Samaria, F. and Harter, A. (1994). Parameterization of a stochastic model for human face identification. In *Proc. of IEEE Workshop on Applications of Computer Vision*, pages 138–142, Sarasota, FL, USA. DOI: 10.1109/ACV.1994.341300. 16

Scherer, S., Glodek, M., Layher, G., Schels, M., Schmidt, M., Brosch, T., Tschechne, S., Schwenker, F., Neumann, H., and Palm, G. (2012). A generic framework for the inference of user states in human computer interaction: how patterns of low level communicational cues support complex affective states. *Journal on Multimodal User Interfaces*. DOI: 10.1007/s12193-012-0093-9. 82

Schneiderman, H. and Kanade, T. (2000). A statistical method for 3d object detection applied to faces and cars. In *Proc. IEEE Conference on Computer Vision and Pattern Recognition*. DOI: 10.1109/CVPR.2000.855895. 15

Sebe, N., Lew, M. S., Cohen, I., Sun, Y., Gevers, T., and Huang, T. S. (2004). Authentic facial expression analysis. In *Proc. IEEE Conference on Face and Gesture Recognition*, pages 517–522. DOI: 10.1109/AFGR.2004.1301585. 32

Shakhnarovich, G., Viola, P., and Darrell, T. (2003). Fast pose estimation with parameter-sensitive hashing. In *Proc. IEEEConference on Computer Vision and Pattern Recognition*, pages 750 –757 vol.2. DOI: 10.1109/ICCV.2003.1238424. 44

Shams, L. and Kim, R. (2010). Crossmodal influences on visual perception. *Physics of Life Reviews*, **7**(3), 269–284. DOI: 10.1016/j.plrev.2010.04.006. 69

Shen, X., Hua, G., Williams, L., and Wu, Y. (2011a). Dynamic hand gesture recognition: An exemplar based approach from motion divergence fields. *Image and Vision Computing*. To Appear. DOI: 10.1016/j.imavis.2011.11.003. 40

Shen, X., Hua, G., Williams, L., and Wu, Y. (2011b). Motion divergence fields for dynamic hand gesture recognition. In *Proc. IEEE 9th IEEE Conf. on Automatic Face and Gesture Recognition*, Santa Barbara, CA. DOI: 10.1109/FG.2011.5771447. 40, 41

Shen, X., Hua, G., Williams, L., and Wu, Y. (2011c). Motion divergence fields for dynamic hand gesture recognition. In *Proc. IEEE 9th IEEE Conf. on Automatic Face and Gesture Recognition*, Santa Barbara, CA. DOI: 10.1109/FG.2011.5771447. 55, 60, 61

Shen, X., Hua, G., Williams, L., and Wu, Y. (2012). Dynamic hand gesture recognition: An exemplar based approach from motion divergence fields. *Image and Vision Computing*, **30**(3), 227–235. DOI: 10.1016/j.imavis.2011.11.003. 55, 59, 60, 61

Shi, J. and Tomasi, C. (1994). Good features to track. In *Computer Vision and Pattern Recognition, 1994. Proceedings CVPR '94., 1994 IEEE Computer Society Conference on*, pages 593–600. DOI: 10.1109/CVPR.1994.323794. 53

Shih, S.-W. and Liu, J. (2004). A novel approach to 3-d gaze tracking using stereo cameras. *IEEE Transactions on Systems, Man, and Cybernetics, Part B: Cybernetics*, **34**(1), 234–245. DOI: 10.1109/TSMCB.2003.811128. 38

Shneiderman, B., Plaisant, C., Cohen, M., and Jacobs, S. (2010). *Designing the User Interface: Strategies for Effective Human-Computer Interaction*. Addison-Wesley, 5th edition. 11

Shotton, J., Fitzgibbon, A., Cook, M., Sharp, T., Finocchio, M., Moore, R., Kipman, A., and Blake, A. (2011). Real-time human pose recognition in parts from a single depth image. In *Proc. of IEEE Conf. on Computer Vision and Pattern Recognition*, Colorado Springs, CO. DOI: 10.1007/978-3-642-28661-2_5. 13, 44, 45, 49, 81

Siddiqui, M. and Medioni, G. (2010). Human pose estimation from a single view point, real-time range sensor. In *Computer Vision and Pattern Recognition Workshops (CVPRW), 2010 IEEE Computer Society Conference on*, pages 1–8. DOI: 10.1109/CVPRW.2010.5543618. 45

Sigal, L., Bhatia, S., Roth, S., Black, M., and Isard, M. (2004). Tracking loose-limbed people. In *Proc. IEEE Conference on Computer Vision and Pattern Recognition*, volume 1, pages I–421–I–428 Vol.1. DOI: 10.1109/CVPR.2004.1315063. 44

Sim, T., Baker, S., and Bsat, M. (2003). The cmu pose, illumination, and expression database. *IEEE Transaction on Pattern Analysis and Machine Intelligence*, **25**(12), 1615–1618. DOI: 10.1109/TPAMI.2003.1251154. 17, 18

Simonyan, K., Parkhi, O. M., Vedaldi, A., and Zisserman, A. (2013). Fisher Vector Faces in the Wild. In *British Machine Vision Conferences*. 27, 28, 29

Sodhi, R., Poupyrev, I., Glisson, M., and Israr, A. (2013a). Aireal: Interactive tactile experiences in free air. *To appear, ACM Transactions on Graphics (Proc. SIGGRAPH 2013)*. DOI: 10.1145/2461912.2462007. 71

Sodhi, R. S., Jones, B. R., Forsyth, D., Bailey, B. P., and Maciocci, G. (2013b). Bethere: 3d mobile collaboration with spatial input. In *Proceedings of the SIGCHI Conference on Human Factors in Computing Systems*, CHI '13, pages 179–188, New York, NY, USA. ACM. DOI: 10.1145/2470654.2470679. 78

Song, Z., Ni, B., Guo, D., Sim, T., and Yan, S. (2011). Learning universal multi-view age estimator by video contexts. In *Proc. IEEE International Conference on Computer Vision*, Barcelona, Spain. DOI: 10.1109/ICCV.2011.6126248. 34, 35

Starner, T. and Pentland, A. (1997). Real-time american sign language recognition from video using hidden markov models. In *Motion-Based Recognition*, pages 227–243. Springer. DOI: 10.1007/978-94-015-8935-2_10. 6

Starner, T., Weaver, J., and Pentland, A. (1998). Real-time american sign language recognition using desk and wearable computer based video. *IEEE Trans. on Pattern Analysis and Machine Intelligence*, **20**(12), 1371–1375. DOI: 10.1109/34.735811. 62, 63, 64

Stenger, B., Woodley, T., and Cipolla, R. (2010). A vision-based remote control. In R. Cipolla, S. Battiato, and G. Farinella, editors, *Computer Vision*, volume 285 of *Studies in Computational Intelligence*, pages 233–262. Springer Berlin / Heidelberg. 10.1007/978-3-642-12848-6_9. 48, 49, 51, 52

Striegnitz, K., Lovett, A., and Cassell, J. (2005). Knowledge representation for generating locating gestures in route directions. In *In Proceedings of Workshop on Spatial Language and Dialogue (5th Workshop on Language and Space*. DOI: 10.1093/acprof:oso/9780199554201.001.0001. 82

Suk, H., Sin, B., and Lee, S. (2008). Recognizing hand gestures using dynamic bayesian network. In *Proc. IEEE Conference on Face and Gesture Recognition*. DOI: 10.1109/AFGR.2008.4813342. 55

Sumby, W. H. and Pollack, I. (1954). Visual contribution to speech intelligibility in noise. *The journal of the acoustical society of america*, **26**, 212. DOI: 10.1121/1.1907384. 70

Sung, K. K. and Poggio, T. (1998). Example-based learning for view-based human face detection. *IEEE Trans. on Pattern Analysis Machine Intelligence*, **20**(1), 39–51. DOI: 10.1109/34.655648. 15

Takacs, B. (1998). Comparing face images using the modified hausdorff distance. *Pattern Recognition*, **31**(12), 1873–1880. DOI: 10.1016/S0031-3203(98)00076-4. 16, 18

Tan, K.-H., Kriegman, D. J., and Ahuja, N. (2002). Appearance-based eye gaze estimation. In *Proc. of IEEE Workshop on Applications of Computer Vision*, pages 191–195. 37, 38

Tao, H. and Huang, T. S. (1999). Explanation-based facial motion tracking using a piecewise bezier volume deformation model. In *Proc. IEEEConference on Computer Vision and Pattern Recognition*, volume 1, pages 611–617. DOI: 10.1109/CVPR.1999.787002. 32

Thiemjarus, S., Poomchoompol, P., Methasate, I., and Theeramunkong, T. (2012). Constraints of accelerometer-based range of motion estimation. In *2012 IEEE-EMBS International Conference on Biomedical and Health Informatics*, pages 551–554. DOI: 10.1109/BHI.2012.6211641. 72

Tian, Y.-L., Kanade, T., and Cohn, J. F. (2005). *Handbook of Face Recognition*, chapter Facial Expression Analysis, pages 247–276. Springer. 32

Tong, Y., Liao, W., and Ji, Q. (2007). Facial action unit recognition by exploiting their dynamic and semantic relationships. *Pattern Analysis and Machine Intelligence, IEEE Transactions on*, **29**(10), 1683–1699. DOI: 10.1109/TPAMI.2007.1094. 32

Toyama, K. (1998). 'look, ma — no hands!' hands-free cursor control with real-time 3d face tracking. In *Proc. Workshop on Perceptual User Interfaces (PUI'98)*, pages 49–54, San francisco. 52

Tran, D. and Forsyth, D. A. (2007). Configuration estimates improve pedestrian finding. Proc. Neural Information Processing Systems. 42

Tu, J., Tao, H., and Huang, T. (2007). Face as mouse through visual face tracking. *Comput. Vis. Image Underst.*, **108**(1-2), 35–40. DOI: 10.1016/j.cviu.2006.11.007. 52, 53, 54

Turk, M. (1998). Moving from guis to puis. In *Proceedings of Fourth Symposium on Intelligent Information Media*. 6, 11

Turk, M. and Kölsch, M. (2004). Perceptual interfaces. *Emerging Topics in Computer Vision, Prentice Hall*. 6, 67

Turk, M. and Pentland, A. (1991a). Eigenfaces for recognition. *Journal of Cognitive Neuroscience*, **3**(1), 71–86. DOI: 10.1162/jocn.1991.3.1.71. 6, 81

Turk, M. A. and Pentland, A. P. (1991b). Face recognition using eigenfaces. In *Proc. of IEEE Conf. on Computer Vision and Patter Recognition*, pages 586–591. DOI: 10.1109/CVPR.1991.139758. 16

Tuzel, O., Porikli, F., and Meer, P. (2007). Human detection via classification on riemannian manifold. Proc. IEEEConference on Computer Vision and Pattern Recognition. 42, 43

Urtasun, R. and Darrell, T. (2008). Sparse probabilistic regression for activity-independent human pose inference. In *Proc. IEEEConference on Computer Vision and Pattern Recognition*, pages 1–8. DOI: 10.1109/CVPR.2008.4587360. 44

Valstar, M., Pantic, M., and Patras, I. (2004). Motion history for facial action detection in video. In *IEEE International Conf. on Systems, Man and Cybernetics*, volume 1, pages 635–640. DOI: 10.1109/ICSMC.2004.1398371. 32

Valstar, M., Mehu, M., Jiang, B., Pantic, M., and Scherer, K. (2012). Meta-analysis of the first facial expression recognition challenge. *Systems, Man, and Cybernetics, Part B: Cybernetics, IEEE Transactions on*, **42**(4), 966–979. DOI: 10.1109/TSMCB.2012.2200675. 33

Valstar, M. F., Gunes, H., and Pantic, M. (2007). How to distinguish posed from spontaneous smiles using geometric features. In *Proc. The 9th International Conference on Multimodal Interfaces*, pages 38–45. DOI: 10.1145/1322192.1322202. 32

Van Dam, A. (1997). Post-wimp user interfaces. *Communications of the ACM*, **40**(2), 63–67. DOI: 10.1145/253671.253708. 6

Vatikiotis-Bateson, E. and Kuratate, T. (2012). Overview of audiovisual speech processing. *Acoustical Science and Technology*, **33**(3), 135–141. DOI: 10.1250/ast.33.135. 70

Vedaldi, A. and Fulkerson, B. (2010). Vlfeat: an open and portable library of computer vision algorithms. In *ACM Multimedia*, pages 1469–1472. DOI: 10.1145/1873951.1874249. 28

Viola, P., Platt, J. C., and Zhang, C. (2005). Multiple instance boosting for object detection. Proc. Neural Information Processing Systems. 43

Viola, P. A. and Jones, M. J. (2001). Rapid object detection using a boosted cascade of simple features. In *Proc. IEEE Conf. on Computer Vision and Pattern Recognition*, volume 1, pages 511–518, Kauai, Hawaii. DOI: 10.1109/CVPR.2001.990517. 12, 15, 16, 17, 39, 51, 52, 81

Vogler, C. and Metaxas, D. (2001). A framework for recognizing the simultaneous aspects of american sign language. *Computer Vision and Image Understanding*, **81**(3), 358–384. DOI: 10.1006/cviu.2000.0895. 62, 64, 65

Vogler, C. and Metaxas, D. N. (1998). Asl recognition based on a coupling between hmms and 3d motion analysis. In *ICCV*, pages 363–369. DOI: 10.1109/ICCV.1998.710744. 62, 63, 64

Vogler, C. and Metaxas, D. N. (1999). Toward scalability in asl recognition: Breaking down signs into phonemes. In *Gesture Workshop*, pages 211–224. 62

Wachs, J. P., Kölsch, M., Stern, H., and Edan, Y. (2011). Vision-based hand-gesture applications. *Communications of ACM*, **54**(2), 60–72. DOI: 10.1145/1897816.1897838. 40, 41, 47

Wang, J. and Canny, J. (2006). Tinymotion: camera phone based interaction methods. In *CHI '06 Extended Abstracts on Human Factors in Computing Systems*, CHI EA '06, pages 339–344, New York, NY, USA. ACM. DOI: 10.1145/1125451.1125526. 61

Wang, J., Yin, L., Wei, X., and Sun, Y. (2006a). 3d facial expression recognition based on primitive surface feature distribution. In *Proc. IEEE Conference on Computer Vision and Pattern Recognition*, pages 1399–1406. DOI: 10.1109/CVPR.2006.14. 32

Wang, P., Green, M. B., Ji, Q., and Wayman, J. (2005). Automatic eye detection and its validation. In *IEEE Workshop on Face Recognition Grand Challenge Experiments*. in Conjunction with CVPR. DOI: 10.1109/CVPR.2005.570. 35, 37

Wang, S. and He, S. (2013). Spontaneous facial expression recognition by fusing thermal infrared and visible images. In *Intelligent Autonomous Systems 12*, pages 263–272. Springer. DOI: 10.1007/978-3-642-33932-5_25. 71

Wang, S., Quattoni, A., Morency, L. P., Demirdjian, D., and Darrell, T. (2006b). Hidden conditional random fields for gesture recognition. In *Proc. IEEE Conference on Computer Vision and Pattern Recognition*. DOI: 10.1109/CVPR.2006.132. 55, 56, 59

Wang, S., Liu, Z., Lv, S., Lv, Y., Wu, G., Peng, P., Chen, F., and Wang, X. (2010). A natural visible and infrared facial expression database for expression recognition and emotion inference. *IEEE Transactions on Multimedia*, **12**(7), 682–691. DOI: 10.1109/TMM.2010.2060716. 71

Wang, X., Han, T. X., and Yan, S. (2009). An hog-lbp human detector with partial occlusion handling. In *IEEE 12th International Conference on Computer Vision*, pages 32–39. DOI: 10.1109/ICCV.2009.5459207. 42

Wang, Y., Yang, C., Wu, X., Xu, S., and Li, H. (2012). Kinect based dynamic hand gesture recognition algorithm research. In *Intelligent Human-Machine Systems and Cybernetics (IHMSC), 2012 4th International Conference on*, volume 1, pages 274–279. DOI: 10.1109/IHMSC.2012.76. 41

Weenk, D., van Beijnum, B.-J. F., Baten, C. T., Hermens, H. J., and Veltink, P. H. (2013). Automatic identification of inertial sensor placement on human body segments during walking. *Journal of Neuroengineering and Rehabilitation*, **10**(1), 31. DOI: 10.1186/1743-0003-10-31. 72

Wen, Z. and Huang, T. S. (2003). Capturing subtle facial motions in 3d face tracking. In *Proc. IEEE International Conference on Computer Vision*, volume 2, pages 1343–1350. DOI: 10.1109/ICCV.2003.1238646. 32

Whitehill, J. and Omlin, C. W. (2006). Haar features for facs au recognition. In *Proc. IEEE Conference on Face and Gesture Recognition*, pages 217–222. DOI: 10.1109/FGR.2006.61. 32

Wiskott, L., Fellous, J.-M., Krüger, N., and von der Malsburg, C. (1997). Face recognition by elastic bunch graph matching. *IEEE Trans. Pattern Analysis Machine Intelligence*, **19**(7), 775–779. DOI: 10.1109/34.598235. 16

Wolf, L. and Levy, N. (2013). The svm-minus similarity score for video face recognition. In *Proc. IEEEConference on Computer Vision and Pattern Recognition*. 30, 31

Wolf, L., Hassner, T., and Taigman, Y. (2008a). Descriptor based methods in the wild. In *Faces in Real-Life Images Workshop in European Conference on Computer Vision (ECCV)*. 16, 17

Wolf, L., Hassner, T., and Taigman, Y. (2008b). Descriptor based methods in the wild. In *Faces in Real-Life Images Workshop in European Conference on Computer Vision (ECCV)*. 29

Wolf, L., Hassner, T., and Maoz, I. (2011). Face recognition in unconstrained videos with matched background similarity. In *Proc. IEEEConference on Computer Vision and Pattern Recognition*, pages 529–534. 17, 27, 28, 29, 30, 31

Wren, C. R., Azarbayejani, A., Darrell, T., and Pentland, A. P. (1997). Pfinder: Real-time tracking of the human body. *Pattern Analysis and Machine Intelligence, IEEE Transactions on*, **19**(7), 780–785. DOI: 10.1109/34.598236. 6

Wright, J. and Hua, G. (2009). Implicit elastic matching with randomized projections for pose-variant face recognition. In *Proc. of IEEE Conf. on Computer Vision and Pattern Recognition*, Miami Beach, FL. DOI: 10.1109/CVPRW.2009.5206786. 16, 17, 19

Wu, B. and Nevatia, R. (2005). Detection of multiple, partially occluded humans in a single image by bayesian combination of edgelet part detectors. Proc. IEEE International Conference on Computer Vision. 42

Wu, B. and Nevatia, R. (2008). Optimizing discrimination-efficientcy tradeoff in integrating heterogeneous local features for object detection. Proc. IEEEConference on Computer Vision and Pattern Recognition. 43

Wu, H.-Y., Rubinstein, M., Shih, E., Guttag, J., Durand, F., and Freeman, W. T. (2012). Eulerian video magnification for revealing subtle changes in the world. *ACM Transactions on Graphics (Proc. SIGGRAPH 2012)*, **31**(4). DOI: 10.1145/2185520.2185561. 78

Wu, Y. and Huang, T. (1999). *Vision-Based Gesture Recognition: A Review*, volume 1739 of *Lecture Notes in Computer Science*, pages 103–115. Springer Berlin Heidelberg. DOI: 10.1007/3-540-46616-9_10. 42

Wu, Y. and Huang, T. S. (2000). View-independent recognition of hand postures. In *Proc. IEEEConference on Computer Vision and Pattern Recognition*, volume 2, pages 88–94. DOI: 10.1109/CVPR.2000.854749. 39

Wu, Y., Liu, Q., and Huang, T. S. (2000). An adaptive self-organizing color segmentation algorithm with application to robust real-time human hand localization. In *Proc. of Asian Conference on Computer Vision*, pages 1106–1111. DOI: 10.1023/A:1008101718719. 39

Wu, Y., Hua, G., and Yu, T. (2003). Tracking articulated body by dynamic markov network. In *Proc. IEEE International Conference on Computer Vision*, pages 1094–1101, Nice,Côte d'Azur,France. DOI: 10.1109/ICCV.2003.1238471. 44

Xiong, X. and la Torre, F. D. (2013). Supervised descent method and its applications to face alignment. In *Proc. IEEEConference on Computer Vision and Pattern Recognition*. 37

Yamato, J., Ohya, J., and Ishii, K. (1992). Recognizing human action in time-sequential images using hidden markov model. In *Proc. IEEEConference on Computer Vision and Pattern Recognition*. DOI: 10.1109/CVPR.1992.223161. 55, 56

Yan, S., Zhou, X., Liu, M., Hasegawa-Johnson, M., and Huang, T. S. (2008). Regression from patch-kernel. In *Proc. IEEEConference on Computer Vision and Pattern Recognition*, pages 1–8. DOI: 10.1109/CVPR.2008.4587405. 35

Yan, S., Wang, H., Fu, Y., Yan, J., Tang, X., and Huang, T. S. (2009). Synchronized submanifold embedding for person-independent pose estimation and beyond. *IEEE Transactions on Image Processing*, **18**(1), 202–210. DOI: 10.1109/TIP.2008.2006400. 34, 35

Yang, C.-M., Hu, J.-S., Yang, C.-W., Wu, C.-C., and Chu, N. (2011). Dancing game by digital textile sensor, accelerometer and gyroscope. In *IEEE International Games Innovation Conference*, pages 121–123. DOI: 10.1109/IGIC.2011.6115112. 72

Yang, M.-H., Roth, D., and Ahuja, N. (2000). A snow-based face detector. In *Advances in Neural Information Processing Systems 12*, pages 855–861. 15

Yang, M. H., Ahuja, N., and Tabb, M. (2002). Extraction of 2d motion trajectories and its application to hand gesture recognition. *IEEE Transactions on Pattern Analysis and Machine Intelligence*, **24**, 1061–1074. DOI: 10.1109/TPAMI.2002.1023803. 56

Ye, G., Corso, J. J., Hager, G. D., and Okamura, A. M. (2003). Vishap: Augmented reality combining haptics and vision. In *International Conference on Systems, Man and Cybernetics*, pages 3425–3431. IEEE. DOI: 10.1109/ICSMC.2003.1244419. 71

Yeasin, M., Bullot, B., and Sharma, R. (2006). Recognition of facial expressions and measurement of levels of interest from video. *IEEE Trans. on Multimedia*, **8**(3), 500–508. DOI: 10.1109/TMM.2006.870737. 33

Yin, L., Wei, X., Sun, Y., Wang, J., and Rosato, M. J. (2006). A 3d facial expression database for facial behavior research. In *Proc. IEEE Conference on Face and Gesture Recognition*, pages 211–216. DOI: 10.1109/FGR.2006.6. 32, 33

Yin, Q., Tang, X., and Sun, J. (2011). An associate-predict model for face recognition. In *Proc. of IEEE Conf. on Computer Vision and Patter Recognition*. DOI: 10.1109/CVPR.2011.5995494. 16, 17

Yin, X. and Zhu, X. (2006). Hand posture recognition in gesture-based human-robot interaction. In *Proc. The 1st IEEE Conference on Industrial Electronics and Applications*, pages 1–6. DOI: 10.1109/ICIEA.2006.257252. 40

Yuille, A. L., Hallinan, P. W., and Cohen, D. S. (1992). Feature extraction from faces using deformable templates. *International journal of computer vision*, **8**(2), 99–111. DOI: 10.1007/BF00127169. 4

Zeng, Z., Pantic, M., Roisman, G. I., and Huang, T. S. (2009). A survey of affect recognition methods: Audio, visual, and spontaneous expressions. *Pattern Analysis and Machine Intelligence, IEEE Transactions on*, **31**(1), 39–58. DOI: 10.1109/TPAMI.2008.52. 13, 31

Zhai, S., Morimoto, C., and Ihde, S. (1999). Manual and gaze input cascaded (magic) pointing. In *Proc. The SIGCHI conference on Human factors in computing systems: the CHI is the limit*, pages 246–253. DOI: 10.1145/302979.303053. 37

Zhang, C. and Zhang, Z. (2010). *Boosting-Based Face Detection and Adaptation*. Synthesis Lectures on Computer Vision. Morgan and Claypool. DOI: 10.2200/S00300ED1V01Y201009COV002. 15, 16

Zhang, Y. and Ji, Q. (2005). Active and dynamic information fusion for facial expression understanding from image sequences. *IEEE Trans. on Pattern Analysis and Machine Intelligence*, **27**(5), 699–714. DOI: 10.1109/TPAMI.2005.93. 32

Zhang, Z., Lyons, M., Schuster, M., and Akamatsu, S. (1998). Comparison between geometry-based and gabor-wavelets-based facial expression recognition using multi-layer perceptron. In *Proc. IEEE Conference on Face and Gesture Recognition*, pages 454–459. DOI: 10.1109/AFGR.1998.670990. 31, 32, 33

Zhao, G., Huang, X., Taini, M., Li, S. Z., and Pietikälnen, M. (2011). Facial expression recognition from near-infrared videos. *Image and Vision Computing*, **29**(9), 607–619. DOI: 10.1016/j.imavis.2011.07.002. 71

Zhen, C., Li, W., Xu, D., Shan, S., and Chen, X. (2013). The svm-minus similarity score for video face recognition. In *Proc. IEEEConference on Computer Vision and Pattern Recognition*. 30, 31

Zhou, X., Cui, N., Li, Z., Liang, F., and Huang, T. (2009). Hierarchical gaussianization for image classification. In *Computer Vision, 2009 IEEE 12th International Conference on*, pages 1971 –1977. DOI: 10.1109/ICCV.2009.5459435. 25

Zhou, Z.-H. and Geng, X. (2004). Projection functions for eye detection. *Pattern Recognition*, **37**(5), 1049–1056. DOI: 10.1016/j.patcog.2003.09.006. 36

Zhu, Q., Avidan, S., Yeh, M.-C., and Cheng, K.-T. (2006). Fast human detection using a cascade of histograms of oriented gradients. Proc. IEEEConference on Computer Vision and Pattern Recognition. 42, 43

Zhu, X. and Ramanan, D. (2012). Face detection, pose estimation, and landmark localization in the wild. In *CVPR*, pages 2879–2886. DOI: 10.1109/CVPR.2012.6248014. 37

Zhu, Y. and Fujimura, K. (2007). Constrained optimization for human pose estimation from depth sequences. In *Proc. of the 8th Asian conference on Computer vision - Volume Part I*, ACCV'07, pages 408–418, Berlin, Heidelberg. Springer-Verlag. DOI: 10.1007/978-3-540-76386-4_38. 45

Zhu, Z. and Ji, Q. (2004). Eye and gaze tracking for interactive graphic display. *Machine Vision and Applications*, **15**, 139–148. DOI: 10.1007/s00138-004-0139-4. 37

Zhu, Z., Ji, Q., Fujimura, K., and Lee, K. (2002). Combining kalman filtering and mean shift for real time eye tracking under active ir illumination. In *International Conference on Pattern Recognition*, volume 4, pages 318 – 321. DOI: 10.1109/ICPR.2002.1047460. 35

Authors' Biographies

MATTHEW TURK

Matthew Turk is a professor of Computer Science and former chair of the Media Arts and Technology program at the University of California, Santa Barbara, where he co-directs the UCSB Four Eyes Lab, focused on the "four I's" of Imaging, Interaction, and Innovative Interfaces. He received a B.S. from Virginia Tech, an M.S. from Carnegie Mellon University, and a Ph.D. from the Massachusetts Institute of Technology. Before joining UCSB in 2000, he worked at Microsoft Research, where he was a founding member of the Vision Technology Group in 1994. He is on the editorial board of the *ACM Transactions on Intelligent Interactive Systems* and the *Journal of Image and Vision Computing*, and he serves on advisory boards for the ACM International Conference on Multimodal Interaction and the IEEE International Conference on Automatic Face and Gesture Recognition. Prof. Turk was a general chair of the 2006 ACM Multimedia Conference and the 2011 IEEE Conference on Automatic Face and Gesture Recognition and is general chair of the upcoming 2014 IEEE Conference on Computer Vision and Pattern Recognition. He has received several best paper awards, most recently at the 2012 International Symposium on Mixed and Augmented Reality (ISMAR). He is an IEEE Fellow and the recipient of the 2011–2012 Fulbright-Nokia Distinguished Chair in Information and Communications Technologies.

GANG HUA

Gang Hua is an Associate Professor of Computer Science at Stevens Institute of Technology. He also currently holds an Academic Advisor position at IBM T. J. Watson Research Center. He was a Consulting Researcher at Microsoft Research in 2012. Before joining Stevens, he had worked as a full-time researcher at leading industrial research labs for IBM, Nokia, and Microsoft. He received the Ph.D. degree in Electrical and Computer Engineering from Northwestern University in 2006. His research in computer vision studies the interconnections and synergies among the visual data, the semantic and situated context, and the users in the expanded physical world, which can be categorized into three themes: human centered visual computing, big visual data analytics, and vision-based cyber-physical systems. He is on the editorial board of *IEEE Transactions on Image*

Processing and the *IAPR Journal of Machine Vision and Applications*. He also served as the lead Guest Editor for *IEEE Transactions on Pattern Recognition and Machine Intelligence* special issue on Real-world Face Recognition, and for *International Journal of Computer Vision* special issue on Mobile Vision. He is the author of more than 60 peer reviewed publications in prestigious international journals and conferences. To date, he holds 9 U.S. patents and has 15 more U.S. patents pending. He is a Senior Member of the IEEE and a life member of the ACM.

Printed in the United States
by Baker & Taylor Publisher Services